"If I lived twenty more years and was able to work, how I should have to modify the *Origin*, and how much the views on all points will have to be modified! Well it is a beginning, and that is something. . . ."

Charles Darwin to J. D. Hooker, 1869

The
AUTOBIOGRAPHY
of
CHARLES
DARWIN

1809–1882

With original omissions restored

Edited with Appendix and Notes
by his grand-daughter, Nora Barlow

W. W. Norton & Company

New York London

Copyright © 1958 by Nora Barlow

First published as a Norton paperback 1969 by arrangement
with Harcourt Brace Jovanovich; reissued 2005

Library of Congress Cataloging-in-Publication Data

Darwin, Charles, 1809–1882.
[Autobiography]
The autobiography of Charles Darwin, 1809–1882 : with original omissions
restored / edited with appendix and notes by his grand-daughter, Nora Barlow.
p. cm.
Originally published: Autobiography. London: Collins, 1958.
Includes index.
ISBN 0-393-31069-8
1. Darwin, Charles, 1809–1882. 2. Evolution (Biology)—History.
3. Naturalists—England—Biography. I. Barlow, Nora. II. Title.
QH31.D2A3   1993
575'.0092—dc20
[B]   93-17940
CIP

W. W. Norton & Company, Inc.
500 Fifth Avenue, New York, N.Y. 10110
www.wwnorton.com

W. W. Norton & Company Ltd.
15 Carlisle Street, London W1D 3BS

Printed in the United States of America

18 • 19 • 20 • 21

PREFACE

In his old age Charles Darwin wrote down his recollections for his own amusement and the interest of his children and their descendants. He finished the main narrative of 121 pages between May and August, 1876, writing as he tells us for an hour on most afternoons. During the last six years of his life he enlarged on what he had already written as fresh memories occurred to him, inserting the sixty-seven further pages of Addenda into their appropriate places. The present edition of the *Autobiography* is a complete transcript of the whole manuscript, now housed in its old leather binding in the Cambridge University Library.

The *Autobiography* first appeared in print as part of *Life and Letters of Charles Darwin* edited by his son Francis and published in 1887 by John Murray, five years after Charles's death, when many omissions were considered necessary.

Two reprints have been published. In 1929 the *Autobiography* was issued as a separate volume in the Thinker's Library, No. 7 (Watts & Co.), with two appendices; the first a chapter of *Reminiscences* by Francis Darwin, and the second a statement also by Francis Darwin of his father's religious views. In 1950 Henry Schuman, New York, issued a volume entitled *Charles Darwin's Autobiography*, which included an introductory essay by G. G. Simpson, *The Meaning of Darwin*; the *Reminiscences* by Francis Darwin, and *Notes and Letters of Charles Darwin depicting the growth of the Origin of Species*. All these texts were taken from the 1887 version, with no revision from the original manuscript. Some excerpts, however, from the unpublished passages have recently appeared, now that the manuscript is available to students.

I have followed the original closely, restoring omissions amounting to nearly six thousand words, and correcting many trivial errors and alterations that had crept into the earlier rendering; and where necessary I have changed erratic punctuation and filled in purely formal abbreviations, both of which checked smooth reading. Throughout, Charles Darwin's parentheses are in round brackets; my own additions are indicated by square ones. Footnotes in Francis Darwin's edition of the *Autobiography* are initialed F. D., those added by me are initialed N. B. To maintain the continuity of the text, I have not marked the earlier omissions as they occur, but there is a page and line reference to the more important at the end of the book for those who wish to trace them.

An Appendix and Notes enlarge on matters arising in the text, and include unpublished letters. The Samuel Butler controversy has been given at considerable length in Part Two of the Appendix, where to some it may appear over-emphasised. But I felt that the unpublished letters threw a further light on the complex story, so often misunderstood. Moreover it has a wider interest as the sequel to Charles Darwin's views on the early evolutionists.

My thanks are due to Sir Charles Darwin, who let me keep the bound volume of the manuscript for many months before it was handed over to the Cambridge University Library. The Librarian has allowed me facilities for a final revision and I am indebted to him for his kindness, and to the helpfulness of Mr. R. V. Kerr and to Mr. Pilgrim.

Help has come from many quarters; from my husband and from my sons; from my sister, Mrs. Rees Thomas; and from my cousins, Mrs. Cornford and the late Mrs. Raverat; and from Miss Sybil Fountain, Mr. Argent and Dr. Padel.

CONTENTS

FAMILY TREE OF CHARLES DARWIN

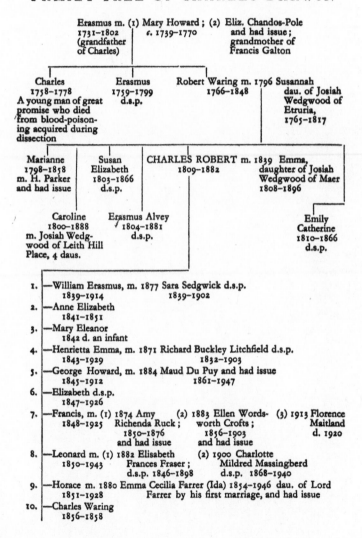

Erasmus m. (1) Mary Howard ; (2) Eliz. Chandos-Pole
1731–1802   *c.* 1739–1770   and had issue ;
(grandfather   grandmother of
of Charles)   Francis Galton

Charles   Erasmus   Robert Waring m. 1796 Susannah
1758–1778   1759–1799   1766–1848   dau. of Josiah
A young man of great   d.s.p.   Wedgwood of
promise who died   Etruria,
from blood-poison-   1765–1817
ing acquired during
dissection

Marianne   Susan   CHARLES ROBERT m. 1839 Emma,
1798–1858   Elizabeth   1809–1882   daughter of Josiah
m. H. Parker   1803–1866   Wedgwood of Maer
and had issue   d.s.p.   1808–1896

Caroline   Erasmus Alvey   Emily
1800–1888   1804–1881   Catherine
m. Josiah Wedg-   d.s.p.   1810–1866
wood of Leith Hill   d.s.p.
Place, 4 daus.

1. —William Erasmus, m. 1877 Sara Sedgwick d.s.p.
    1839–1914   1839–1902

2. —Anne Elizabeth
    1841–1851

3. —Mary Eleanor
    1842 d. an infant

4. —Henrietta Emma, m. 1871 Richard Buckley Litchfield d.s.p.
    1843–1929   1832–1903

5. —George Howard, m. 1884 Maud Du Puy and had issue
    1845–1912   1861–1947

6. —Elizabeth d.s.p.
    1847–1926

7. —Francis, m. (1) 1874 Amy   (2) 1883 Ellen Words- (3) 1913 Florence
    1848–1925   Richenda Ruck ;   worth Crofts ;   Maitland
                 1850–1876   1856–1903   d. 1920
                 and had issue   and had issue

8. —Leonard m. (1) 1882 Elisabeth   (2) 1900 Charlotte
    1850–1943   Frances Fraser ;   Mildred Massingberd
              d.s.p. 1846–1898   d.s.p. 1868–1940

9. —Horace m. 1880 Emma Cecilia Farrer (Ida) 1854–1946 dau. of Lord
    1851–1928   Farrer by his first marriage, and had issue

10. —Charles Waring
     1856–1858

INTRODUCTION

CHARLES DARWIN'S own reflections on his life and work, written between the ages of 67 and 73, must remain an important work of reference, whether in the history of ideas or in a portrait gallery of men. He still stands as the leading figure of that revolution in scientific thought which followed the publication of the *Origin of Species* in the middle of the 19th century, a revolution soon involving all realms of knowledge. But posterity must continually reassess the past, and accurate contemporary sources are specially needed to provide insight into those stormy seasons when the wind of accepted belief changes. The great figures must be seen in their own setting and their own words must be heard, cleared of the posthumous growth of later dogmas. In the *Autobiography* Charles Darwin tells the story of the slow maturing of his mind and of his theories, leading to the publication of the Linnean paper with A. R. Wallace in 1858, and of the *Origin of Species* in 1859.

The time has come for restoring the suppressions made in 1887. The occasional astringency of some passages had to be censored seventy years ago out of deference to the feelings of friends; now these comments not only seem harmless, but are revealing flashes lighting up the past.

The major suppressions, however, arose from the memory of the intense feelings roused after the publication of the *Origin*, and still alive in the early eighties, when Francis Darwin was working at *Life and Letters*. The family was, in fact, divided concerning the publication of some of the passages relating to Charles Darwin's religious beliefs. Francis, the editor, held the view that complete publication was the right course, whilst other members of the family felt strongly that Charles's views, so privately recorded and not intended for publication, would be damaging to himself in their crudity.

I write as one of the next generation, and it is difficult now to imagine the state of tension that existed in what had always seemed to us a solid and united phalanx of uncles and aunts. Yet soon after Charles's death, before the publication of *Life and Letters*, feelings were so strong that litigation was suggested. Leonard Darwin[1] wrote to me in 1942:—"I am now the only person alive who can remember what hot feelings were aroused at the time about the publication of the *Autobiography*. Etty[2] went so far as to *speak* of legal proceedings to stop its publication. These could only have been against Frank. She felt that on religious questions it was crude and but half thought-out, and that in these circumstances it was not only unfair to his memory to publish it, but that he would have objected strongly. I should not be surprised if my Mother, unknown to us all, put in the final word against it [publication of the suppressed passages] to Frank." The suggestion of Mrs. Darwin's intervention is supported by a comment in her own handwriting in a manuscript copy of the *Autobiography* written out by Francis. This comment is given as a footnote in its appropriate place. The underlining of the word "speak" in Leonard's letter shows, I think, that he felt sure that Henrietta, his sister, would never have taken legal action. Nevertheless it is clear that opinions were divided and feelings ran high in this united family, perhaps best explained by a divided loyalty amongst the children between the science of their father and the religion of their mother; though the differences of view that

[1] Charles Darwin's fourth son, became a Major in the Royal Engineers.
[2] Henrietta, Charles's eldest daughter, married R. B. Litchfield.

existed caused no estrangement between the parents. This desire for reticence was an aftermath of the scientific-religious storm that had raged in the 60's and 70's with a fury that is now difficult to understand. Charles's own shrinking from anything verging on public or personal dispute, also found an echo in this family difference after his death. Francis refers to Charles's religion and to his reticence in Chap. VIII of *Life and Letters*, Vol. I, considerable parts of which are drawn from the *Autobiography*,— passages which were presumably passed by the family censorship, and which are here reinstated in their right place.

Evolution has now been widely accepted, and the author of the *Origin of Species* has been dead for over seventy years. Omissions that were made so soon after his death should now be replaced, for all available evidence is of value concerning those who transform fundamental beliefs; how fundamental the change was it is difficult to remember to-day, when it is hard to think back into the pre-evolutionary era.

It is true that the coming of evolution had a long history behind it; and there are those who would place Charles Darwin as a kind of lucky number in this lineage of over two thousand years. The unsubstantiated theory was in the air;—the time was ripe; and so on. But the time is always ripe for the re-interpretation of theories in the light of new vision and of new facts. This is the very province of science. Darwin's whole trend of thought was against facile speculation, yet theories flowed freely through his mind ready for the essential tests of observation and experiment. He took twenty years of combined theorizing and fact-finding to prepare his case for evolution in the face of a predominantly antagonistic world. He had to convince himself by accumulated evidence before he could convince others, and his doubts are as freely expressed as his convictions. His books lie like stepping-stones to future knowledge. Dogmatic fixity was wholly alien to his central idea.

Later discoveries have not undermined Darwin's position. Mendelian genetics and advances in the studies of cytology and

variation have rather confirmed and supported the main theme of
the *Origin of Species*, so that his name remains more closely linked
than any other with the admission of evolutionary beliefs into
nineteenth-century orthodoxy. In the *Autobiography* he is seen
taking his place in the historic procession, and much is revealed
beyond the conscious statements. We can see the picture of the
Darwin-Wedgwood ancestry, both as genetic forebears and as
representatives of the Utilitarian and Whig traditions. We can
watch his dominating love of natural history changing from his
youthful passion for collecting and shooting, into the maturer
passion of the theoriser; we can watch his diffidence slowly giving way to scientific assurance, though never to dogmatic final-
ity. In the later editions of the *Origin* Darwin showed an
increasing belief in the inheritance of acquired characters and in
the importance of use and disuse in the total picture of evolution,
which led to some ambiguity of expression as to their respective
roles in relation to Natural Selection.[3] Darwin's faith in Natural
Selection as the main agent never wavered, but this admission of
other causes showed his awareness of difficulties still unsolved;
indeed his vacillations may prove his wisdom in the light of
recent work.[4]

The passage from the *Autobiography* reproduced in facsimile
opposite, demonstrates these doubts, and shows how his thoughts
jostled each other for priority, leading to additions and excisions.
The passage occurs on p. 74.

True portraits of great men in their settings are specially
needed at this time; for two schools of thought incline to take the
figures of history and mould them into demonstrations of their
own doctrines. To the Marxian the individual man is made by his
economic environment; the revolutionary, the artist, the inventor,

---

[3] See C. Darlington's reprint of the first edition of the *Origin*, Watts & Co. 1950.
[4] See C. Waddington, *Principles of Embryology*, 1956.

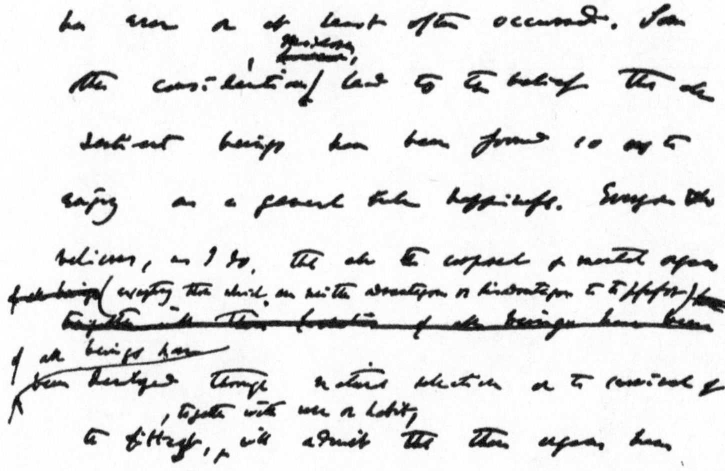

is pushed up like a bubble out of the seething economic need. The Freudian likewise, though on very different grounds, puts the genetic endowment at a discount, and sees a man's achievement from the point of view of his adjustment or maladjustment to his particular experience. Doubtless both aspects have their validity, for there is no development for man without environment, both of the body and the mind. Self-portraits have the merit of disclosing the influences as well as the man. There may be some to whom the *Autobiography* will prove what Charles Darwin was not—a metaphysician or profound thinker beyond the scope of his world-wide subject. But no one can read his own words and fail to recognise a character of rare simplicity and complete integrity. The *Autobiography* shows how it was that he altered the whole course of Victorian thought, not by blazoning his discoveries nor by sudden iconoclasm, but rather through searching insight and pondered judgments opening up vast fields for further research.

The

AUTOBIOGRAPHY

Table of Contents

May 31st, 1876
Recollections of the Development of
my mind and character

A GERMAN EDITOR having written to me to ask for an account of the development of my mind and character with some sketch of my autobiography, I have thought that the attempt would amuse me, and might possibly interest my children or their children. I know that it would have interested me greatly to have read even so short and dull a sketch of the mind of my grandfather written by himself, and what he thought and did and how he worked. I have attempted to write the following account of myself, as if I were a dead man in another world looking back at my own life. Nor have I found this difficult, for life is nearly over with me. I have taken no pains about my style of writing.

I was born at Shrewsbury on February 12th, 1809. I have heard my Father say that he believed that persons with powerful minds generally had memories extending far back to a very early period of life. This is not my case for my earliest recollection goes back only to when I was a few months over four years old, when we went to near Abergele for sea-bathing, and I recollect some events and places there with some little distinctness.

My mother died in July 1817, when I was a little over eight years old, and it is odd that I can remember hardly anything about her except her death-bed, her black velvet gown, and her curiously constructed work-table. I believe that my forgetfulness is partly due to my sisters, owing to their great grief, never being able to speak about her or mention her name; and partly to her previous invalid state. In the spring of this same year I was sent to a day-school in Shrewsbury,[1] where I staid a year. Before going to school I was educated by my sister Caroline, but I doubt whether this plan answered. I have been told that I was much slower in learning than my younger sister Catherine, and I believe that I was in many ways a naughty boy. Caroline was extremely kind, clever and zealous; but she was too zealous in trying to improve me; for I clearly remember after this long interval of years, saying to myself when about to enter a room where she was—"What will she blame me for now?" and I made myself dogged so as not to care what she might say.

By the time I went to this day-school my taste for natural history, and more especially for collecting, was well developed. I tried to make out the names of plants, and collected all sorts of things, shells, seals, franks, coins, and minerals. The passion for collecting, which leads a man to be a systematic naturalist, a virtuoso or a miser, was very strong in me, and was clearly innate, as none of my sisters or brother ever had this taste.

One little event during this year has fixed itself very firmly in my mind, and I hope that it has done so from my conscience having been afterwards sorely troubled by it; it is curious as showing that apparently I was interested at this early age in the variability of plants! I told another little boy (I believe it was Leighton,[2] who afterwards became a well-known Lichenologist and botanist) that I could produce variously coloured Polyanthuses and Primroses by

---

[1] Kept by Rev. G. Case, minister of the Unitarian Chapel in the High Street. Mrs. Darwin was a Unitarian and attended Mr. Case's chapel, and my father as a little boy went there with his elder sisters. But both he and his brother were christened and intended to belong to the Church of England; and after his early boyhood he seems usually to have gone to church and not to Mr. Case's. It appears (*St. James's Gazette*, December 15, 1883) that a mural tablet has been erected to his memory in the chapel, which is now known as the "Free Christian Church."—F. D.

[2] Rev. W. A. Leighton, who was a schoolfellow of my father's at Mr. Case's school, remembers his bringing a flower to school and saying that his mother

watering them with certain coloured fluids, which was of course a monstrous fable, and had never been tried by me. I may here also confess that as a little boy I was much given to inventing deliberate falsehoods, and this was always done for the sake of causing excitement. For instance, I once gathered much valuable fruit from my Father's trees and hid them in the shrubbery, and then ran in breathless haste to spread the news that I had discovered a hoard of stolen fruit.[3]

About this time, or as I hope at a somewhat earlier age, I sometimes stole fruit for the sake of eating it; and one of my schemes was ingenious. The kitchen garden was kept locked in the evening, and was surrounded by a high wall, but by the aid of neighbouring trees I could easily get on the coping. I then fixed a long stick into the hole at the bottom of a rather large flower-pot, and by dragging this upwards pulled off peaches and plums, which fell into the pot and the prizes were thus secured. When a very little boy I remember stealing apples from the orchard, for the sake of giving them away to some boys and young men who lived in a cottage not far off, but before I gave them the fruit I showed off how quickly I could run and it is wonderful that I did not perceive that the surprise and admiration which they expressed at my powers of running, was given for the sake of the apples. But I well remember that I was delighted at them declaring that they had never seen a boy run so fast!

---

had taught him how by looking at the inside of the blossom the name of the plant could be discovered. Mr. Leighton goes on, "This greatly roused my attention and curiosity, and I inquired of him repeatedly how this could be done?"— but his lesson was naturally enough not transmissible.—F. D. William Allport Leighton (1805–1899), botanist, educated at St. John's College, Cambridge; published *Flora of Shropshire*, *Lichen Flora of Great Britain*, and other works.— N. B.

[3] His Father wisely treated this tendency not by making crimes of the fibs, but by making light of the discoveries.—F. D.

I remember clearly only one other incident during the years whilst at Mr. Case's daily school—namely, the burial of a dragoon-soldier; and it is surprising how clearly I can still see the horse with the man's empty boots and carbine suspended to the saddle, and the firing over the grave. This scene deeply stirred whatever poetic fancy there was in me.[4]

In the summer of 1818 I went to Dr. Butler's great school in Shrewsbury, and remained there for seven years till Mid-summer 1825, when I was sixteen years old. I boarded at this school, so that I had the great advantage of living the life of a true school-boy; but as the distance was hardly more than a mile to my home, I very often ran there in the longer intervals between the callings over and before locking up at night. This I think was in many ways advantageous to me by keeping up home affections and interests. I remember in the early part of my school life that I often had to run very quickly to be in time, and from being a fleet runner was generally successful; but when in doubt I prayed earnestly to God to help me, and I well remember that I attributed my success to the prayers and not to my quick running, and marvelled how generally I was aided.

I have heard my father and elder sisters say that I had, as a very young boy, a strong taste for long solitary walks; but what I thought about I know not. I often became quite absorbed, and once, whilst returning to school on the summit of the old fortifications round Shrewsbury, which had been converted into a public foot-path with no parapet on one side, I walked off and fell to

[4] It is curious that another Shrewsbury boy should have been impressed by this military funeral; Mr. Gretton, in his *Memory's Harkback*, says that the scene is so strongly impressed on his mind that he could "walk straight to the spot in St. Chad's churchyard where the poor fellow was buried." The soldier was an Inniskilling Dragoon, and the officer in command had been recently wounded at Waterloo, where his corps did good service against the French Cuirassiers.—F. D.

the ground, but the height was only seven or eight feet. Nevertheless the number of thoughts which passed through my mind during this very short, but sudden and wholly unexpected fall, was astonishing, and seem hardly compatible with what physiologists have, I believe, proved about each thought requiring quite an appreciable amount of time.

I must have been a very simple little fellow when I first went to the school. A boy of the name of Garnett took me into a cakeshop one day, and bought some cakes for which he did not pay, as the shopman trusted him. When we came out I asked him why he did not pay for them, and he instantly answered, "Why, do you not know that my uncle left a great sum of money to the Town on condition that every tradesman should give whatever was wanted without payment to anyone who wore his old hat and moved it in a particular manner"; and he then showed me how it was moved. He then went into another shop where he was trusted, and asked for some small article, moving his hat in the proper manner, and of course obtained it without payment. When we came out he said, "Now if you like to go by yourself into that cake-shop (how well I remember its exact position), I will lend you my hat, and you can get whatever you like if you move the hat on your head properly." I gladly accepted the generous offer, and went in and asked for some cakes, moved the old hat, and was walking out of the shop, when the shopman made a rush at me, so I dropped the cakes and ran away for dear life, and was astonished by being greeted with shouts of laughter by my false friend Garnett.

I can say in my own favour that I was as a boy humane, but I owed this entirely to the instruction and example of my sisters. I doubt indeed whether humanity is a natural or innate quality. I was very fond of collecting eggs, but I never took more than a single egg out of a bird's nest, except on one single occasion, when I took all, not for their value, but from a sort of bravado.

I had a strong taste for angling, and would sit for any number of hours on the bank of a river or pond watching the float; when at Maer[5] I was told that I could kill the worms with salt and water, and from that day I never spitted a living worm, though at the expense, probably, of some loss of success.

Once as a very little boy, whilst at the day-school, or before that time, I acted cruelly, for I beat a puppy I believe, simply from enjoying the sense of power; but the beating could not have been severe, for the puppy did not howl, of which I feel sure as the spot was near to the house. This act lay heavily on my conscience, as is shown by my remembering the exact spot where the crime was committed. It probably lay all the heavier from my love of dogs being then, and for a long time afterwards, a passion. Dogs seemed to know this, for I was an adept in robbing their love from their masters.

Nothing could have been worse for the development of my mind than Dr. Butler's school, as it was strictly classical, nothing else being taught except a little ancient geography and history. The school as a means of education to me was simply a blank. During my whole life I have been singularly incapable of mastering any language. Especial attention was paid to verse-making, and this I could never do well. I had many friends, and got together a grand collection of old verses, which by patching together, sometimes aided by other boys, I could work into any subject. Much attention was paid to learning by heart the lessons of the previous day; this I could effect with great facility learning forty or fifty lines of Virgil or Homer, whilst I was in morning chapel; but this exercise was utterly useless, for every verse was forgotten in forty-eight hours. I was not idle, and with the excep-

---

[5] The house of his uncle, Josiah Wedgwood, the younger.—F. D. Here lived a family of Wedgwood cousins, the youngest of whom became Charles's wife. Maer lay in the heart of the Shropshire country, only a 20-miles' ride from Shrewsbury.—N. B.

tion of versification, generally worked conscientiously at my classics, not using cribs. The sole pleasure I ever received from such
studies, was from some of the odes of Horace, which I admired
greatly. When I left the school I was for my age neither high nor
low in it; and I believe that I was considered by all my masters
and by my Father as a very ordinary boy, rather below the common standard in intellect. To my deep mortification my father
once said to me, "You care for nothing but shooting, dogs, and
rat-catching, and you will be a disgrace to yourself and all your
family." But my father, who was the kindest man I ever knew, and
whose memory I love with all my heart, must have been angry
and somewhat unjust when he used such words.

I may here add a few pages about my Father, who was in many
ways a remarkable man.[6]

He was about 6 feet 2 inches in height, with broad shoulders,
and very corpulent, so that he was the largest man whom I ever
saw. When he last weighed himself, he was 24 stone, but afterwards increased much in weight. His chief mental characteristics
were his powers of observation and his sympathy, neither of which
have I ever seen exceeded or even equalled. His sympathy was not
only with the distresses of others, but in a greater degree with the
pleasures of all around him. This led him to be always scheming
to give pleasure to others, and, though hating extravagance, to
perform many generous actions. For instance, Mr. B———, a
small manufacturer in Shrewsbury, came to him one day, and said
he should be bankrupt unless he could at once borrow £10,000,
but that he was unable to give any legal security. My father heard
his reasons for believing that he could ultimately repay the
money, and from my Father's intuitive perception of character felt

[6] This addition (ending p. 38) was written in 1878 or later, and though
included in *Life and Letters*, Vol. I, p. 11, it was omitted in the *Autobiography* of
the Thinker's Library.—N. B.

sure that he was to be trusted. So he advanced this sum, which was a very large one for him while young, and was after a time repaid.

I suppose that it was his sympathy which gave him unbounded power of winning confidence, and as a consequence made him highly successful as a physician. He began to practise before he was twenty-one years old, and his fees during the first year paid for the keep of two horses and a servant. On the following year his practice was larger, and so continued for above sixty years, when he ceased to attend on any one. His great success as a doctor was the more remarkable, as he told me that he at first hated his profession so much that if he had been sure of the smallest pittance, or if his father had given him any choice, nothing should have induced him to follow it. To the end of his life, the thought of an operation almost sickened him, and he could scarcely endure to see a person bled—a horror which he has transmitted to me—and I remember the horror which I felt as a schoolboy in reading about Pliny (I think) bleeding to death in a warm bath. My Father told me two odd stories about bleeding: one was that as a very young man he became a Freemason. A friend of his who was a Freemason and who pretended not to know about his strong feeling with respect to blood, remarked casually to him as they walked to the meeting, "I suppose that you do not care about losing a few drops of blood?" It seems that when he was received as a member, his eyes were bandaged and his coat-sleeves turned up. Whether any such ceremony is now performed I know not, but my Father mentioned the case as an excellent instance of the power of imagination, for he distinctly felt the blood trickling down his arm, and could hardly believe his own eyes, when he afterwards could not find the smallest prick on his arm.

A great slaughtering butcher from London once consulted my grandfather, when another man very ill was brought in, and my grandfather wished to have him instantly bled by the accompanying apothecary. The butcher was asked to hold the patient's arm, but he made some excuse and left the room. Afterwards he explained to my grandfather that although he believed that he had killed with his own hands more animals than any other man in London, yet absurd as it might seem he assuredly should have fainted if he had seen the patient bled.

Owing to my father's power of winning confidence, many patients, especially ladies, consulted him when suffering from any misery, as a sort of Father-Confessor. He told me that they always began by complaining in a vague manner about their health, and by practice he soon guessed what was really the matter. He then suggested that they had been suffering in their minds, and now they would pour out their troubles, and he heard nothing more about the body. Family quarrels were a common subject. When gentlemen complained to him about their wives, and the quarrel seemed serious, my Father advised them to act in the following manner; and his advice always succeeded if the gentleman followed it to the letter, which was not always the case. The husband was to say to the wife that he was very sorry that they could not live happily together,—that he felt sure that she would be happier if separated from him—that he did not blame her in the least (this was the point on which the man oftenest failed)—that he would not blame her to any of her relations or friends and lastly that he would settle on her as large a provision as he could afford. She was then asked to deliberate on this proposal. As no fault had been found, her temper was unruffled, and she soon felt what an awkward position she would be in, with no accusation to rebut, and with her husband and not herself proposing a separation. Invariably the lady begged her husband not to think of separation, and usually behaved much better ever afterwards.

Owing to my father's skill in winning confidence he received many strange confessions of misery and guilt. He often remarked how many miserable wives he had known. In several instances husbands and wives had gone on pretty well together for between twenty and thirty years, and then hated each other bitterly: this he attributed to their having lost a common bond in their young children having grown up.

But the most remarkable power which my father possessed was that of reading the characters, and even the thoughts of those whom he saw even for a short time. We had many instances of this power, some of which seemed almost supernatural. It saved my father from ever making (with one exception, and the character of this man was soon discovered) an unworthy friend. A strange clergyman came to Shrewsbury, and seemed to be a rich man; everybody called on him, and he was invited to many houses. My father called, and on his return home told my sisters on no account to invite him or his family to our house; for he felt sure that the man was not to be trusted. After a few months he suddenly bolted, being heavily in debt, and was found out to be little better than an habitual swindler. Here is a case of trustfulness which not many men would have ventured on. An Irish gentleman, a complete stranger, called on my father one day, and said that he had lost his purse, and that it would be a serious inconvenience to him to wait in Shrewsbury until he could receive a remittance from Ireland. He then asked my father to lend him £20, which was immediately done, as my father felt certain that the story was a true one. As soon as a letter could arrive from Ireland, one came with the most profuse thanks, and enclosing, as he said, a £20 Bank of England note; but no note was enclosed. I asked my father whether this did not stagger him, but he answered "not in the least." On the next day another letter came with many apologies for having forgotten (like a true Irishman) to put the note into his letter of the day before.

A connection[7] of my Father's consulted him about his son who was strangely idle and would settle to no work. My Father said "I believe that the foolish young man thinks that I shall bequeath

---

[7] Robert's son-in-law, Henry Parker, who had married his eldest daughter, Marianne, in 1824.—N. B.

him a large sum of money. Tell him that I have declared to you that I shall not leave him a penny." The Father of the youth owned with shame that this preposterous idea had taken possession of his son's mind; and he asked my Father how he could possibly have discovered it, but my Father said he did not in the least know.

The Earl of —— brought his nephew, who was insane but quite gentle, to my father; and the young man's insanity led him to accuse himself of all the crimes under heaven. When my Father afterwards talked about the case with the uncle, he said, "I am sure that your nephew is really guilty of . . . a heinous crime." Whereupon the Earl of —— exclaimed, "Good God, Dr. Darwin, who told you; we thought that no human being knew the fact except ourselves!" My Father told me the story many years after the event, and I asked him how he distinguished the true from the false self-accusations; and it was very characteristic of my Father that he said he could not explain how it was.

The following story shows what good guesses my Father could make. Lord Sherburn,[8] afterwards the first Marquis of Lansdowne, was famous (as Macaulay somewhere remarks) for his knowledge of the affairs of Europe, on which he greatly prided himself. He consulted my Father medically, and afterwards harangued him on the state of Holland. My father had studied medicine at Leyden, and one day went a long walk into the country with a friend, who took him to the house of a clergyman (we will say the Rev. Mr. A——, for I have forgotten his name), who had married an Englishwoman. My father was very hungry, and there was little for luncheon except cheese, which he could never eat. The old lady was surprised and grieved at this, and assured my father that it was an excellent cheese, and had been sent her from Bowood, the seat of Lord Sherburn. My father wondered why a cheese should be sent her from Bowood, but thought nothing more about it until it flashed across his mind many years afterwards, whilst Lord

[8] Read "Shelburne," consistently mis-spelt whenever mentioned.—N. B.

Sherburn was talking about Holland. So he answered, "I should think from what I saw of the Rev. Mr. A——, that he was a very able man and well acquainted with the state of Holland." My father saw that the Earl, who immediately changed the conversation, was much startled. On the next morning my father received a note from the Earl, saying that he had delayed starting on his journey, and wished particularly to see my father. When he called, the Earl said, "Dr. Darwin, it is of the utmost importance to me and to the Rev. Mr. A—— to learn how you have discovered that he is the source of my information about Holland." So my father had to explain the state of the case, and he supposed that Lord Sherburn was much struck with his diplomatic skill in guessing, for during many years afterwards he received many kind messages from him through various friends. I think that he must have told the story to his children; for Sir C. Lyell asked me many years ago why the Marquis of Lansdowne (the son or grandson of the first marquis) felt so much interest about me, whom he had never seen, and my family. When forty new members (the forty thieves as they were then called) were added to the Athenæum Club, there was much canvassing to be one of them; and without my having asked any one, Lord Lansdowne proposed me and got me elected. If I am right in my supposition, it was a queer concatenation of events that my father not eating cheese half-a-century before in Holland led to my election as a member of the Athenæum.

Early in life my father occasionally wrote down a short account of some curious event and conversation, which are enclosed in a separate envelope.

The sharpness of his observation led him to predict with remarkable skill the course of any illness, and he suggested endless small details of relief. I was told that a young Doctor in Shrewsbury, who disliked my father, used to say that he was wholly unscientific, but owned that his power of predicting the end of an illness was unparalleled. Formerly when he thought that I should be a doctor, he talked much to me about his patients. In the old

days the practice of bleeding largely was universal, but my father
maintained that far more evil was thus caused than good done; and
he advised me if ever I was myself ill not to allow any doctor to
take from me more than an extremely small quantity of blood.
Long before typhoid fever was recognised as distinct, my father
told me that two utterly distinct kinds of illness were confounded
under the name of typhus fever. He was vehement against drinking, and was convinced of both the direct and inherited evil effects
of alcohol when habitually taken even in moderate quantity in a
very large majority of cases.[9] But he admitted and advanced
instances of certain persons, who could drink largely during their
whole lives without apparently suffering any evil effects; and he
believed that he could often beforehand tell who would thus not
suffer. He himself never drank a drop of any alcoholic fluid. This
remark reminds me of a case showing how a witness under the
most favourable circumstances may be wholly mistaken. A
gentleman-farmer was strongly urged by my father not to drink,
and was encouraged by being told that he himself never touched
any spirituous liquor. Whereupon the gentleman said, "Come,
come, Doctor, that won't do—though it is very kind of you to say
so for my sake—for I know that you take a very large glass of hot
gin and water every evening after your dinner."[10] So my father asked
him how he knew this. The man answered, "My cook was your
kitchen-maid for two or three years, and she saw the butler every
day prepare and take to you the gin and water." The explanation
was that my father had the odd habit of drinking hot water in a
very tall and large glass after his dinner; and the butler used first
to put some cold water in the glass, which the girl mistook for gin,
and then filled it up with boiling water from the kitchen boiler.

[9] See Note 1. p. 187 This letter from Robert's father, Dr. Erasmus Darwin, dis-
cusses the question of drink.—N. B.
[10] This belief still survives, and was mentioned to my brother in 1884 by an old
inhabitant of Shrewsbury.—F. D.

My father used to tell me many little things which he had found useful in his medical practice. Thus ladies often cried much while telling him their troubles, and thus caused much loss of his precious time. He soon found that begging them to command and restrain themselves, always made them weep the more, so that afterwards he always encouraged them to go on crying, saying that this would relieve them more than anything else, with the invariable result that they soon ceased to cry, and he could hear what they had to say and give his advice. When patients who were very ill, craved for some strange and unnatural food, my father asked them what had put such an idea into their heads: if they answered that they did not know, he would allow them to try the food, and often with success, as he trusted to their having a kind of instinctive desire; but if they answered that they had heard that the food in question had done good to someone else, he firmly refused his assent.

He gave one day an odd little specimen of human nature. When a very young man he was called in to consult with the family physician in the case of a gentleman of much distinction in Shropshire. The old doctor told the wife that the illness was of such a nature that it must end fatally. My father took a different view and maintained that the gentleman would recover: he was proved quite wrong in all respects, (I think by autopsy) and he owned his error. He was then convinced that he should never again be consulted by this family; but after a few months the widow sent for him, having dismissed the old family doctor. My father was so much surprised at this, that he asked a friend of the widow to find out why he was again consulted. The widow answered her friend, that "she would never again see that odious old doctor who said from the first that her husband would die, while Dr. Darwin always maintained that he would recover!" In another case my father told a lady that her husband would certainly die. Some months afterwards he saw the widow who was a very sensible woman, and she said, "You are a very young man, and allow me to advise you always to give, as long as you possibly can, hope to any near relation nursing a patient. You made me despair, and from that moment I lost strength." My father said that he had often since seen the paramount importance, for the sake of the patient, of keeping up the hope and with it the strength of the nurse in charge. This he sometimes found it difficult to do compatibly with truth. One old gentleman, however, Mr. Pemberton, caused him no such perplexity. He was sent for by Mr. Pemberton, who said, "From all that I have seen and heard of you I believe you are the sort of man who will speak the truth, and if I ask you will tell me when I am dying. Now I much desire that you should attend me, if you will promise, whatever I may say, always to declare that I am not going to die." My father acquiesced on this understanding that his words should in fact have no meaning.

My father possessed an extraordinary memory, especially for dates, so that he knew, when he was very old the day of the birth, marriage, and death of a multitude of persons in Shropshire; and he once told me that this power annoyed him; for if he once heard a date he could not forget it; and thus the deaths of many friends were often recalled to his mind. Owing to his strong memory he knew an extraordinary number of curious stories, which he liked to tell, as he was a great talker. He was generally in high spirits, and laughed and joked with every one—often with his servants— with the utmost freedom; yet he had the art of making every one obey him to the letter. Many persons were much afraid of him. I remember my father telling us one day with a laugh, that several persons had asked him whether Miss Piggott (a grand old lady in Shropshire), had called on him, so that at last he enquired why they asked him; and was told that Miss Piggott, whom my father had somehow mortally offended, was telling everybody that she would call and tell "that fat old doctor very plainly what she thought of him." She had already called, but her courage had failed, and no one could have been more courteous and friendly.

As a boy, I went to stay at the house of Major B———, whose wife was insane; and the poor creature, as soon as she saw me, was in the most abject state of terror that I ever saw, weeping bitterly and asking me over and over again, "Is your father coming?" but was soon pacified. On my return home, I asked my father why she was so frightened, and he answered he [was] very glad to hear it, as he had frightened her on purpose, feeling sure that she could be kept in safety and much happier without any restraint, if her husband could influence her, whenever she became at all violent, by proposing to send for Dr. Darwin; and these words succeeded perfectly during the rest of her long life.

My father was very sensitive so that many small events annoyed or pained him much. I once asked him, when he was old and could not walk, why he did not drive out for exercise; and he answered, "Every road out of Shrewsbury is associated in my mind with some painful event." Yet he was generally in high spirits. He was easily made very angry, but as his kindness was unbounded, he was widely and deeply loved.

He was a cautious and good man of business, so that he hardly ever lost money by any investment, and left to his children a very large property. I remember a story, showing how easily utterly false beliefs originate and spread. Mr. E———, a squire of one of the oldest families in Shropshire, and head partner in a Bank, committed suicide. My father was sent for as a matter of form, and found him dead. I may mention by the way, to show how matters were managed in those old days, that because Mr. E——— was a rather great man and universally respected, no inquest was held over his body. My father, in returning home, thought it proper to call at the Bank (where he had an account) to tell the managing partner of the event, as it was not improbable it would cause a run on the bank. Well the story was spread far and wide, that my father went into the bank, drew out all his money, left the bank, came back again, and said, "I may just tell you that Mr. E———has killed himself," and then departed. It seems that it was then a common belief that money withdrawn from a bank was not safe, until the person had passed out through the door of the bank. My father did not hear this story till some little time afterwards, when the managing partner said that he had departed from his invariable rule of never allowing any one to see the account of another man, by having shown the ledger with my father's account to several persons, as this proved that my father had not drawn out a penny on that day. It would have been dishonourable in my father to have used his professional knowledge for his private advantage. Nevertheless the supposed act was greatly admired by some persons; and many years afterwards, a gentleman remarked, "Ah, Doctor, what a splendid man of business you were in so cleverly getting all your money safe out of that bank." My father's mind was not scientific, and he did not try to generalise his knowledge under general laws; yet he formed a theory for almost everything which occurred. I do not think that I gained much from him intellectually; but his example ought to have been of much moral service to all his children. One of his golden rules (a hard one to follow) was, "Never become the friend of any one whom you cannot respect."

With respect to my Father's father, the author of the *Botanic Garden* etc., I have put together all the facts which I could collect in his published *Life*.[11]

Having said this much about my Father, I will add a few words about my brother and sisters.

My brother Erasmus possessed a remarkably clear mind, with extensive and diversified tastes and knowledge in literature, art, and even in science. For a short time he collected and dried plants, and during a somewhat longer time experimented in chemistry. He was extremely agreeable, and his wit often reminded me of that in the letters and works of Charles Lamb. He was very kind-hearted; but his health from his boyhood had been weak, and as a

[11] See Appendix, Part 1. p. 121, on Dr. Erasmus Darwin.

consequence he failed in energy. His spirits were not high, sometimes low, more especially during early and middle manhood. He
read much, even whilst a boy, and at school encouraged me to
read, lending me books. Our minds and tastes were, however, so
different that I do not think that I owe much to him intellectually—nor to my four sisters, who possessed very different characters, and some of them had strongly marked characters. All were
extremely kind and affectionate towards me during their whole
lives. I am inclined to agree with Francis Galton in believing that
education and environment produce only a small effect on the
mind of any one, and that most of our qualities are innate.

The above sketch of my brother's character was written before
that which was published in Carlyle's Remembrances, and which
appears to me to have little truth and no merit.

Looking back as well as I can at my character during my
school life, the only qualities which at this period promised well
for the future, were, that I had strong and diversified tastes,
much zeal for whatever interested me, and a keen pleasure in
understanding any complex subject or thing. I was taught Euclid
by a private tutor, and I distinctly remember the intense satisfaction which the clear geometrical proofs gave me. I remember
with equal distinctness the delight which my uncle gave me (the
father of Francis Galton) by explaining the principle of the
vernier of a barometer. With respect to diversified tastes, independently of science, I was fond of reading various books, and I
used to sit for hours reading the historical plays of Shakespeare,
generally in an old window in the thick walls of the school. I read
also other poetry, such as the recently published poems of Byron,
Scott, and Thomson's *Seasons*. I mention this because later in life
I wholly lost, to my great regret, all pleasure from poetry of any
kind, including Shakespeare. In connection with pleasure from
poetry I may add that in 1822 a vivid delight in scenery was first
awakened in my mind, during a riding tour on the borders of

Wales, and which has lasted longer than any other aesthetic pleasure.

Early in my school-days a boy had a copy of the *Wonders of the World*, which I often read and disputed with other boys about the veracity of some of the statements; and I believe this book first gave me a wish to travel in remote countries, which was ultimately fulfilled by the voyage of the *Beagle*. In the latter part of my school life I became passionately fond of shooting, and I do not believe that anyone could have shown more zeal for the most holy cause than I did for shooting birds. How well I remember killing my first snipe, and my excitement was so great that I had much difficulty in reloading my gun from the trembling of my hands. This taste long continued and I became a very good shot. When at Cambridge I used to practise throwing up my gun to my shoulder before a looking-glass to see that I threw it up straight. Another and better plan was to get a friend to wave about a lighted candle, and then to fire at it with a cap on the nipple, and if the aim was accurate the little puff of air would blow out the candle. The explosion of the cap caused a sharp crack, and I was told that the Tutor of the College remarked, "What an extraordinary thing it is, Mr. Darwin seems to spend hours in cracking a horse-whip in his room, for I often hear the crack when I pass under his windows."

I had many friends amongst the schoolboys, whom I loved dearly, and I think that my disposition was then very affectionate. Some of these boys were rather clever, but I may add on the principle of "noscitur a socio" that not one of them ever became in the least distinguished.

With respect to science, I continued collecting minerals with much zeal, but quite unscientifically—all that I cared for was a new *named* mineral, and I hardly attempted to classify them. I must have observed insects with some little care, for when ten years old (1819) I went for three weeks to Plas Edwards on the sea-coast in Wales, I was very much interested and surprised at seeing a large black and scarlet Hemipterous insect, many moths

(Zygæna) and a Cicindela, which are not found in Shropshire. I almost made up my mind to begin collecting all the insects which I could find dead, for on consulting my sister, I concluded that it was not right to kill insects for the sake of making a collection. From reading White's *Selborne* I took much pleasure in watching the habits of birds, and even made notes on the subject. In my simplicity I remember wondering why every gentleman did not become an ornithologist.

Towards the close of my school life, my brother worked hard at chemistry and made a fair laboratory with proper apparatus in the tool-house in the garden, and I was allowed to aid him as a servant in most of his experiments. He made all the gases and many compounds, and I read with care several books on chemistry, such as Henry and Parkes' *Chemical Catechism*. The subject interested me greatly, and we often used to go on working till rather late at night. This was the best part of my education at school, for it showed me practically the meaning of experimental science. The fact that we worked at chemistry somehow got known at school, and as it was an unprecedented fact, I was nicknamed "Gas." I was also once publicly rebuked by the head-master, Dr. Butler, for thus wasting my time over such useless subjects; and he called me very unjustly a "poco curante," and as I did not understand what he meant it seemed to me a fearful reproach.

As I was doing no good at school, my father wisely took me away at a rather earlier age than usual, and sent me (October 1825) to Edinburgh University[12] with my brother, where I stayed for two years or sessions. My brother was completing his medical studies, though I do not believe he ever really intended to prac-

[12] He lodged at Mrs. Mackay's, 11 Lothian Street. What little the records of Edinburgh University can reveal has been published in the *Edinburgh Weekly Dispatch*, May 22, 1888; and in the *St. James's Gazette*, February 16, 1888. From the latter journal it appears that he and his brother Erasmus made more use of the library than was usual among the students of their time.—F. D.

tice, and I was sent there to commence them. But soon after this period I became convinced from various small circumstances that my father would leave me property enough to subsist on with some comfort, though I never imagined that I should be so rich a man as I am; but my belief was sufficient to check any strenuous effort to learn medicine.

The instruction at Edinburgh was altogether by Lectures, and these were intolerably dull, with the exception of those on chemistry by Hope;[13] but to my mind there are no advantages and many disadvantages in lectures compared with reading. Dr. Duncan's lectures on Materia Medica at 8 o'clock on a winter's morning are something fearful to remember. Dr. Munro made his lectures on human anatomy as dull, as he was himself, and the subject disgusted me. It has proved one of the greatest evils in my life that I was not urged to practise dissection, for I should soon have got over my disgust; and the practice would have been invaluable for all my future work. This has been an irremediable evil, as well as my incapacity to draw. I also attended regularly the clinical wards in the Hospital. Some of the cases distressed me a good deal, and I still have vivid pictures before me of some of them; but I was not so foolish as to allow this to lessen my attendance. I cannot understand why this part of my medical course did not interest me in a greater degree; for during the summer before coming to Edinburgh I began attending some of the poor people, chiefly children and women in Shrewsbury: I wrote down as full an account as I could of the cases with all the symptoms, and read them aloud to my father, who suggested further enquiries, and advised me what medicines to give, which I made up myself. At one time I had at least a dozen patients, and I felt a keen interest in the work.[14] My father, who was by far the best

[13] Thomas Charles Hope, 1766–1844, Professor of Chemistry at Edinburgh, 1799–1843.—N. B.
[14] I have heard him call to mind the pride he felt at the results of the successful treatment of a whole family with tartar emetic.—F. D.

judge of character whom I ever knew, declared that I should make a successful physician,—meaning by this, one who got many patients. He maintained that the chief element of success was exciting confidence; but what he saw in me which convinced him that I should create confidence I know not. I also attended on two occasions the operating theatre in the hospital at Edinburgh, and saw two very bad operations, one on a child, but I rushed away before they were completed. Nor did I ever attend again, for hardly any inducement would have been strong enough to make me do so; this being long before the blessed days of chloroform. The two cases fairly haunted me for many a long year.

My Brother staid only one year at the University, so that during the second year I was left to my own resources; and this was an advantage, for I became well acquainted with several young men fond of natural science. One of these was Ainsworth,[15] who afterwards published his travels in Assyria: he was a Wernerian[16] geologist and knew a little about many subjects, but was superficial and very glib with his tongue. Dr. Coldstream[17] was a very different young man, prim, formal, highly religious and most kind-hearted: he afterwards published some good zoological articles. A third young man was Hardie, who would I think have made a good botanist, but died early in India. Lastly, Dr. Grant,[18] my senior by several years, but how I became acquainted with him I can-

[15] William Francis Ainsworth, 1807–1896, L.R.C.S., Edinburgh 1827. Studied geology in London, Paris and Brussels. Surgeon and geologist to expedition to Euphrates, 1835; led expedition to Christians of Chaldea, 1838–40.—N. B.

[16] Abraham Gottlob Werner, 1750–1817, geologist; adherent of the Neptunian theory—that all rocks were deposited as precipitates from water.—N. B.

[17] Dr. Coldstream died September 17, 1863; see Crown 16mo. Book Tract, No. 19, of the Religious Tract Society (no date).—F. D. This footnote is given in the Thinker's Library Edition, not in *Life and Letters*.—N. B.

[18] Robert Edmund Grant, 1793–1874, Professor of comparative anatomy and zoology at London University 1827–1874; F.R.S. 1836. T. H. Huxley writes of Grant thus:—"Within the ranks of the biologists at that time (1851–8) I met

not remember: he published some first-rate zoological papers, but after coming to London as Professor in University College, he did nothing more in science—a fact which has always been inexplicable to me. I knew him well; he was dry and formal in manner, but with much enthusiasm beneath this outer crust. He one day, when we were walking together burst forth in high admiration of Lamarck and his views on evolution. I listened in silent astonishment, and as far as I can judge, without any effect on my mind. I had previously read the *Zoönomia* of my grandfather, in which similar views are maintained, but without producing any effect on me. Nevertheless it is probable that the hearing rather early in life such views maintained and praised may have favoured my upholding them under a different form in my *Origin of Species*. At this time I admired greatly the *Zoönomia*; but on reading it a second time after an interval of ten or fifteen years, I was much disappointed, the proportion of speculation being so large to the facts given.[19]

Drs. Grant and Coldstream attended much to marine Zoology, and I often accompanied the former to collect animals in the tidal pools, which I dissected as well as I could. I also became friends with some of the Newhaven fishermen, and sometimes accompanied them when they trawled for oysters, and thus got many specimens. But from not having had any regular practice in dissection, and from possessing only a wretched microscope my attempts were very poor. Nevertheless I made one interesting little discovery, and read about the beginning of the year 1826, a short paper on the subject before the Plinian Socy. This was that the so-called ova of Flustra had the power of independent movement by means of cilia, and were in fact larvæ. In another short paper I showed that little globular bodies which had been supposed to be the young state of *Fucus loreus* were the egg-cases of the worm-like *Pontobdella muricata*.

---

nobody, except Dr. Grant, of University College who had a word to say for Evolution;—and his advocacy was not calculated to advance the cause." *Life and Letters*, Vol. II, p. 188.—N. B.

[19] See Appendix Part 1, on Dr. Erasmus Darwin, p. 123.—N. B.

The Plinian Society[20] was encouraged and I believe founded by Professor Jameson:[21] it consisted of students and met in an underground room in the University for the sake of reading papers on natural science and discussing them. I used regularly to attend and the meetings had a good effect on me in stimulating my zeal and giving me new congenial acquaintances. One evening a poor young man got up and after stammering for a prodigious length of time, blushing crimson, he at last slowly got out the words, "Mr. President, I have forgotten what I was going to say." The poor fellow looked quite overwhelmed, and all the members were so surprised that no one could think of a word to say to cover his confusion. The papers which were read to our little society were not printed, so that I had not the satisfaction of seeing my paper in print; but I believe Dr. Grant noticed my small discovery in his excellent memoir on Flustra.

I was also a member of the Royal Medical Society, and attended pretty regularly, but as the subjects were exclusively medical I did not much care about them. Much rubbish was talked there, but there were some good speakers, of whom the best was the present Sir J. Kay-Shuttleworth.[22] Dr. Grant took me occasionally to the meetings of the Wernerian Society, where various papers on natural history were read, discussed, and afterwards published in the Transactions. I heard Audubon[23] deliver there

---

[20] The society was founded in 1823, and expired about 1848 (*Edinburgh Weekly Dispatch*, May 22, 1888).—F. D.

[21] Robert Jameson, 1774–1854, Regius professor of natural history and Keeper of the Museum at Edinburgh 1804–1854. Founded the Wernerian Society, 1808.—N. B.

[22] James Phillips Kay-Shuttleworth, 1st Baronet, 1804–1877, M.D., Edinburgh, 1827; Assistant Poor-law Commissioner 1835; first Secretary of the Committee of Council of Education, 1839–49; member of scientific commissions, etc.—N. B.

[23] John James Audubon, 1780–1851. Ornithologist and author of *The Birds of America*, and *The Quadrupeds of North America*.—N. B.

some interesting discourses on the habits of N. American birds, sneering somewhat unjustly at Waterton.[24] By the way, a negro lived in Edinburgh, who had travelled with Waterton and gained his livelihood by stuffing birds, which he did excellently; he gave me lessons for payment, and I used often to sit with him, for he was a very pleasant and intelligent man.

Mr. Leonard Horner[25] also took me once to a meeting of the Royal Society of Edinburgh, where I saw Sir Walter Scott in the chair as President, and he apologised to the meeting as not feeling fitted for such a position. I looked at him and at the whole scene with some awe and reverence; and I think it was owing to this visit during my youth and to my having attended the Royal Medical Society, that I felt the honour of being elected a few years ago an honorary member of both these Societies, more than any other similar honour. If I had been told at that time that I should one day have been thus honoured, I declare that I should have thought it as ridiculous and improbable, as if I had been told that I should be elected King of England.

During my second year in Edinburgh I attended Jameson's lectures on Geology and Zoology, but they were incredibly dull. The sole effect they produced on me was the determination never as long as I lived to read a book on Geology or in any way to study the science. Yet I feel sure that I was prepared for a philosophical treatment of the subject; for an old Mr. Cotton in Shropshire who knew a good deal about rocks, had pointed out to me, two or three years previously a well-known large erratic boulder in the town of Shrewsbury, called the bell-stone; he told me that there was no rock of the same kind nearer than Cumberland or Scotland, and he solemnly assured me that the world would come to an end

[24] Charles Waterton, 1782–1865. Naturalist and traveller, author of *Wanderings in S. America.*—N. B.
[25] Leonard Horner, 1785–1864. Geologist and educationalist; helped to organise London Institution, 1827; took active part in Factory Acts.—N. B.

before anyone would be able to explain how this stone came where it now lay. This produced a deep impression on me and I meditated over this wonderful stone. So that I felt the keenest delight when I first read of the action of icebergs in transporting boulders, and I gloried in the progress of Geology. Equally striking is the fact that I, though now only sixty-seven years old, heard Professor Jameson, in a field lecture at Salisbury Craigs, discoursing on a trap-dyke, with amygdaloidal margins and the strata indurated on each side, with volcanic rocks all around us, and say that it was a fissure filled with sediment from above, adding with a sneer that there were men who maintained that it had been injected from beneath in a molten condition. When I think of this lecture, I do not wonder that I determined never to attend to Geology.

From attending Jameson's lectures, I became acquainted with the curator of the museum, Mr. Macgillivray,[26] who afterwards published a large and excellent book on the birds of Scotland. He had not much the appearance or manners of the gentleman. I had much interesting natural-history talk with him, and he was very kind to me. He gave me some rare shells, for I at that time collected marine mollusca, but with no great zeal.

My summer vacations during these two years were wholly given up to amusements, though I always had some book in hand, which I read with interest. During the summer of 1826, I took a long walking tour with two friends with knapsacks on our backs through North Wales. We walked thirty miles most days, including one day the ascent of Snowdon. I also went with my sister Caroline a riding tour in North Wales, a servant with saddle-bags carrying our clothes. The autumns were devoted to shooting, chiefly at Mr. Owen's at Woodhouse, and at my Uncle Jos's,[27] at Maer. My zeal was so great that I used to place my

[26] William Macgillivray, 1796–1852. Conservator of the Royal College of Surgeons Museum, Edinburgh, 1831–41. Professor of Natural History, Aberdeen, 1841. Author of *A History of British Birds*.—N. B.

[27] Josiah Wedgwood, the son of the founder of the Etruria Works.—F. D.

shooting boots open by my bed-side when I went to bed, so as not to lose half-a-minute in putting them on in the morning; and on one occasion I reached a distant part of the Maer estate on the 20th of August for black-game shooting, before I could see: I then toiled on with the gamekeeper the whole day through thick heath and young Scotch firs. I kept an exact record of every bird which I shot throughout the whole season. One day when shooting at Woodhouse with Captain Owen, the eldest son and Major Hill, his cousin, afterwards Lord Berwick, both of whom I liked very much, I thought myself shamefully used, for every time after I had fired and thought that I had killed a bird, one of the two acted as if loading his gun and cried out, "You must not count that bird, for I fired at the same time," and the gamekeeper perceiving the joke, backed them up. After some hours they told me the joke, but it was no joke to me for I had shot a large number of birds, but did not know how many, and could not add them to my list, which I used to do by making a knot in a piece of string tied to a button-hole. This my wicked friends had perceived.

How I did enjoy shooting, but I think that I must have been half-consciously ashamed of my zeal, for I tried to persuade myself that shooting was almost an intellectual employment; it required so much skill to judge where to find most game and to hunt the dogs well.

One of my autumnal visits to Maer in 1827 was memorable from meeting there Sir J. Mackintosh,[28] who was the best converser I ever listened to. I heard afterwards with a glow of pride that he had said, "There is something in that young man that interests me." This must have been chiefly due to his perceiving that I listened with much interest to everything which he said,

---

[28] Sir James Mackintosh, 1765–1832, philosopher and historian. Had studied medicine at Edinburgh. He and Josiah Wedgwood of Maer married two of the Allen sisters, so there was connection by marriage between the families.—N. B.

for I was as ignorant as a pig about his subjects of history, politicks and moral philosophy. To hear of praise from an eminent person, though no doubt apt or certain to excite vanity, is, I think, good for a young man, as it helps to keep him in the right course.

My visits to Maer during these two and the three succeeding years were quite delightful, independently of the autumnal shooting. Life there was perfectly free; the country was very pleasant for walking or riding; and in the evening there was much very agreeable conversation, not so personal as it generally is in large family parties, together with music. In the summer the whole family used often to sit on the steps of the old portico, with the flower-garden in front, and with the steep wooded bank, opposite the house, reflected in the lake, with here and there a fish rising or a water-bird paddling about. Nothing has left a more vivid picture on my mind than these evenings at Maer. I was also attached to and greatly revered my Uncle Jos: he was silent and reserved so as to be a rather awful man; but he sometimes talked openly with me.[29] He was the very type of an upright man with the clearest judgment. I do not believe that any power on earth could have made him swerve an inch from what he considered the right course. I used to apply to him in my mind, the well-known ode of Horace, now forgotten by me, in which the words "nec vultus tyranni, &c.,"[30] come in.

---

[29] Sydney Smith was a frequent visitor at Maer, and Mrs. Litchfield quotes her mother's memory of a speech of his:—"Wedgwood's an excellent man—it is a pity he hates his friends." *Emma Darwin*, Vol. I, p. 74.—N. B.

[30] Justum et tenacem propositi virum
  Non civium ardor prava jubentium,
  Non vultus instantis tyranni
  Mente quatit solida.   F. D.

Cambridge, 1828–1831

AFTER HAVING spent two sessions in Edinburgh, my father perceived or he heard from my sisters, that I did not like the thought of being a physician, so he proposed that I should become a clergyman. He was very properly vehement against my turning an idle sporting man, which then seemed my probable destination. I asked for some time to consider, as from what little I had heard and thought on the subject I had scruples about declaring my belief in all the dogmas of the Church of England; though otherwise I liked the thought of being a country clergyman. Accordingly I read with care *Pearson on the Creed* and a few other books on divinity; and as I did not then in the least doubt the strict and literal truth of every word in the Bible, I soon persuaded myself that our Creed must be fully accepted. It never struck me how illogical it was to say that I believed in what I could not understand and what is in fact unintelligible. I might have said with entire truth that I had no wish to dispute any dogma; but I never was such a fool as to feel and say "credo quia incredibile."

Considering how fiercely I have been attacked by the orthodox it seems ludicrous that I once intended to be a clergyman. Nor was this intention and my father's wish ever formally given up, but died a natural death when on leaving Cambridge I joined the *Beagle* as Naturalist. If the phrenologists are to be trusted, I was well fitted in one respect to be a clergyman. A few years ago the Secretaries of a German psychological society asked me earnestly by letter for a photograph of myself; and some time afterwards I received the proceedings of one of the meetings in which it seemed that the shape of my head had been the subject of a public discussion, and one of the speakers declared that I had the bump of Reverence developed enough for ten Priests.

As it was decided that I should be a clergyman, it was necessary that I should go to one of the English universities and take a degree; but as I had never opened a classical book since leaving school, I found to my dismay that in the two intervening years I had actually forgotten, incredible as it may appear, almost everything which I had learnt even to some few of the Greek letters. I did not therefore proceed to Cambridge at the usual time in October, but worked with a private tutor in Shrewsbury and went to Cambridge after the Christmas vacation, early in 1828. I soon recovered my school standard of knowledge, and could translate easy Greek books, such as Homer and the Greek Testament with moderate facility.

During the three years which I spent at Cambridge my time was wasted, as far as the academical studies were concerned, as completely as at Edinburgh and at school. I attempted mathematics, and even went during the summer of 1828 with a private tutor (a very dull man) to Barmouth, but I got on very slowly. The work was repugnant to me, chiefly from my not being able to see any meaning in the early steps in algebra. This impatience was very foolish, and in after years I have deeply regretted that I did not proceed far enough at least to understand something of the great leading principles of mathematics; for men thus endowed seem to have an extra sense. But I do not believe that I should ever have succeeded beyond a very low grade. With respect to Classics I did nothing except attend a few compulsory college lectures, and the attendance was almost nominal. In my second year I had to work for a month or two to pass the Little Go, which I did easily. Again in my last year I worked with some earnestness for my final degree of B.A., and brushed up my Classics together with a little Algebra and Euclid, which latter gave me much pleasure, as it did whilst at school. In order to pass the B.A. examination, it was, also, necessary to get up Paley's *Evidences of Christianity*, and his *Moral Philosophy*. This was done in a thorough manner, and I am convinced that I could have written out the whole of the *Evi-*

dences with perfect correctness, but not of course in the clear language of Paley. The logic of this book and as I may add of his *Natural Theology* gave me as much delight as did Euclid. The careful study of these works, without attempting to learn any part by rote, was the only part of the Academical Course which, as I then felt and as I still believe, was of the least use to me in the education of my mind. I did not at that time trouble myself about Paley's premises; and taking these on trust I was charmed and convinced by the long line of argumentation. By answering well the examination questions in Paley, by doing Euclid well, and by not failing miserably in Classics, I gained a good place among the οἱ πολλοί, or crowd of men who do not go in for honours. Oddly enough I cannot remember how high I stood, and my memory fluctuates between the fifth, tenth, or twelfth name on the list.[31]

Public lectures on several branches were given in the University, attendance being quite voluntary; but I was so sickened with lectures at Edinburgh that I did not even attend Sedgwick's[32] eloquent and interesting lectures. Had I done so I should probably have become a geologist earlier than I did. I attended, however, Henslow's[33] lectures on Botany, and liked them much for their extreme clearness, and the admirable illustrations; but I did not study botany. Henslow used to take his pupils, including several of the older members of the University, field excursions, on foot, or in coaches to distant places, or in a barge down the river, and lectured on the rarer plants or animals which were observed. These excursions were delightful.

Although as we shall presently see there were some redeeming features in my life at Cambridge, my time was sadly wasted there

[31] Tenth in the list of January 1831.—F. D.

[32] Adam Sedgwick, 1785–1873. Woodwardian professor of geology, Cambridge, 1818. F.R.S., 1830.—N. B.

[33] John Stevens Henslow, 1796–1861. Professor of botany, Cambridge, 1827–61. He helped to obtain for Darwin the post of naturalist on the *Beagle*, and Darwin always held him in very high esteem.—N. B.

and worse than wasted. From my passion for shooting and for hunting and when this failed, for riding across country I got into a sporting set, including some dissipated low-minded young men. We used often to dine together in the evening, though these dinners often included men of a higher stamp, and we sometimes drank too much, with jolly singing and playing at cards afterwards. I know that I ought to feel ashamed of days and evenings thus spent, but as some of my friends were very pleasant and we were all in the highest spirits, I cannot help looking back to these times with much pleasure.[34]

But I am glad to think that I had many other friends of a widely different nature. I was very intimate with Whitley,[35] who was afterwards Senior Wrangler, and we used continually to take long walks together. He inoculated me with a taste for pictures and good engravings, of which I bought some. I frequently went to the Fitzwilliam Gallery, and my taste must have been fairly good, for I certainly admired the best pictures, which I discussed with the old curator. I read also with much interest Sir J. Reynolds' book. This taste, though not natural to me, lasted for several years and many of the pictures in the National Gallery in London gave me much pleasure; that of Sebastian del Piombo exciting in me a sense of sublimity.

I also got into a musical set, I believe by means of my warm-hearted friend Herbert,[36] who took a high wrangler's degree. From associating with these men and hearing them play, I acquired a strong taste for music, and used very often to time my walks so as to hear on week days the anthem in King's College

[34] I gather from some of my father's contemporaries that he has exaggerated the Bacchanalian nature of these parties.—F. D.
[35] Rev. C. Whitley, Hon. Canon of Durham, formerly Reader in Natural Philosophy in Durham University.—F. D.
[36] The late John Maurice Herbert, County Court Judge of Cardiff and the Monmouth Circuit.—F. D.

Chapel. This gave me intense pleasure, so that my backbone would sometimes shiver. I am sure that there was no affectation or mere imitation in this taste, for I used generally to go by myself to King's College, and I sometimes hired the chorister boys to sing in my rooms. Nevertheless I am so utterly destitute of an ear, that I cannot perceive a discord, or keep time and hum a tune correctly; and it is a mystery how I could possibly have derived pleasure from music.

My musical friends soon perceived my state, and sometimes amused themselves by making me pass an examination, which consisted in ascertaining how many tunes I could recognise, when they were played rather more quickly or slowly than usual. "God save the King" when thus played was a sore puzzle. There was another man with almost as bad an ear as I had, and strange to say he played a little on the flute. Once I had the triumph of beating him in one of our musical examinations.

But no pursuit at Cambridge was followed with nearly so much eagerness or gave me so much pleasure as collecting beetles. It was the mere passion for collecting, for I did not dissect them and rarely compared their external characters with published descriptions, but got them named anyhow. I will give a proof of my zeal: one day, on tearing off some old bark, I saw two rare beetles and seized one in each hand; then I saw a third and new kind, which I could not bear to lose, so that I popped the one which I held in my right hand into my mouth. Alas it ejected some intensely acrid fluid, which burnt my tongue so that I was forced to spit the beetle out, which was lost, as well as the third one.

I was very successful in collecting and invented two new methods; I employed a labourer to scrape during the winter, moss off old trees and place [it] in a large bag, and likewise to collect the rubbish at the bottom of the barges in which reeds are brought from the fens, and thus I got some very rare species. No poet ever felt more delight at seeing his first poem published than I did at seeing in Stephen's *Illustrations of British Insects* the magic words, "captured by C. Darwin, Esq." I was introduced to entomology by my second cousin, W. Darwin Fox, a clever and most pleasant man, who was then at Christ's College, and with whom I became extremely intimate. Afterwards I became well acquainted with and went out collecting, with Albert Way[37] of Trinity, who in after years became a well-known archæologist; also with H. Thompson,[38] of the same College, afterwards a leading agriculturist, chairman of a great Railway, and Member of Parliament. It seems therefore that a taste for collecting beetles is some indication of future success in life!

I am surprised what an indelible impression many of the beetles which I caught at Cambridge have left on my mind. I can remember the exact appearance of certain posts, old trees and banks where I made a good capture. The pretty *Panagæus crux-major* was a treasure in those days, and here at Down I saw a beetle running across a walk, and on picking it up instantly perceived that it differed slightly from *P. crux-major*, and it turned out to be *P. quadripunctatus*, which is only a variety or closely allied species, differing from it very slightly in outline. I had never seen in those old days Licinus alive, which to an uneducated eye hardly differs from many other black Carabidous beetles; but my sons found here a specimen and I instantly recognised that it was new to me; yet I had not looked at a British beetle for the last twenty years.

I have not as yet mentioned a circumstance which influenced my whole career more than any other. This was my friendship with Prof. Henslow. Before coming up to Cambridge, I had heard of him from my brother as a man who knew every branch of science, and I was accordingly prepared to reverence him. He kept

[37] Albert Way, 1805–74. Antiquarian, traveller and editor of *Promptorium Parvulorum*, 1843–65.—N. B.

[38] Afterwards Sir H. Thompson, first baronet.—F. D.

open house once every week,[39] where all undergraduates and several older members of the University, who were attached to science, used to meet in the evening. I soon got, through Fox, an invitation, and went there regularly. Before long I became well acquainted with Henslow, and during the latter half of my time at Cambridge took long walks with him on most days; so that I was called by some of the dons "the man who walks with Henslow"; and in the evening I was very often asked to join his family dinner. His knowledge was great in botany, entomology, chemistry, mineralogy, and geology. His strongest taste was to draw conclusions from long-continued minute observations. His judgment was excellent, and his whole mind well-balanced; but I do not suppose that anyone would say that he possessed much original genius.

He was deeply religious, and so orthodox, that he told me one day, he should be grieved if a single word of the Thirty-nine Articles were altered. His moral qualities were in every way admirable. He was free from every tinge of vanity or other petty feeling; and I never saw a man who thought so little about himself or his own concerns. His temper was imperturbably good, with the most winning and courteous manners; yet, as I have seen, he could be roused by any bad action to the warmest indignation and prompt action. I once saw in his company in the streets of Cambridge almost as horrid a scene, as could have been witnessed during the French Revolution. Two body-snatchers had been arrested and whilst being taken to prison had been torn from the constable by a crowd of the roughest men, who dragged them by their legs along the muddy and stony road. They were covered from head to foot with mud and their faces were bleeding either from having been kicked or from the stones; they looked like corpses, but the crowd was so

[39] The *Cambridge Ray Club*, which in 1887 attained its fiftieth anniversary, is the direct descendant of these meetings, having been founded to fill the blank caused by the discontinuance, in 1836, of Henslow's Friday evenings. See Professor Babington's pamphlet, *The Cambridge Ray Club*, 1887.—F. D.

dense that I got only a few momentary glimpses of the wretched creatures. Never in my life have I seen such wrath painted on a man's face, as was shown by Henslow at this horrid scene. He tried repeatedly to penetrate the mob; but it was simply impossible. He then rushed away to the mayor, telling me not to follow him, to get more policemen. I forget the issue, except that the two were got into the prison before being killed.

Henslow's benevolence was unbounded, as he proved by his many excellent schemes for his poor parishioners, when in after years he held the living of Hitcham. My intimacy with such a man ought to have been and I hope was an inestimable benefit. I cannot resist mentioning a trifling incident, which showed his kind consideration. Whilst examining some pollen-grains on a damp surface I saw the tubes exserted, and instantly rushed off to communicate my surprising discovery to him. Now I do not suppose any other Professor of Botany could have helped laughing at my coming in such a hurry to make such a communication. But he agreed how interesting the phenomenon was, and explained its meaning, but made me clearly understand how well it was known; so I left him not in the least mortified, but well pleased at having discovered for myself so remarkable a fact, but determined not to be in such a hurry again to communicate my discoveries.

Dr. Whewell[40] was one of the older and distinguished men who sometimes visited Henslow, and on several occasions I walked home with him at night. Next to Sir J. Mackintosh he was the best converser on grave subjects to whom I ever listened. Leonard Jenyns,[41] (grandson of the famous Soames Jenyns), who afterwards published some good essays in Natural History, often staid with Henslow, who was his brother-in-law. At first I disliked him from his somewhat grim and sarcastic expression; and it is not often that

[40] William Whewell, 1794–1866, Master of Trinity College, Cambridge, 1841–1866. F.R.S. 1820. Philosopher, theologian and scientist.—N. B.
[41] Mr. Jenyns (now Blomefield) described the fish for the *Zoology of the Voyage of H.M.S. Beagle*; and is author of a long series of papers, chiefly zoological. In 1887

a first impression is lost; but I was completely mistaken and found him very kind-hearted, pleasant and with a good stock of humour. I visited him at his parsonage on the borders of the Fens [Swaffham Bulbeck], and had many a good walk and talk with him about Natural History. I became also acquainted with several other men older than me, who did not care much about science, but were friends of Henslow. One was a Scotchman, brother of Sir Alexander Ramsay, and tutor of Jesus College; he was a delightful man, but did not live for many years. Another was Mr. Dawes, afterwards Dean of Hereford and famous for his success in the education of the poor. These men and others of the same standing, together with Henslow, used sometimes to take distant excursions into the country, which I was allowed to join and they were most agreeable.

Looking back, I infer that there must have been something in me a little superior to the common run of youths, otherwise the above-mentioned men, so much older than me and higher in academical position, would never have allowed me to associate with them. Certainly I was not aware of any such superiority, and I remember one of my sporting friends, Turner, who saw me at work on my beetles, saying that I should some day be a Fellow of the Royal Society, and the notion seemed to me preposterous.

During my last year at Cambridge I read with care and profound interest Humboldt's *Personal Narrative.* This work and Sir J. Herschel's *Introduction to the Study of Natural Philosophy* stirred up in me a burning zeal to add even the most humble contribution to the noble structure of Natural Science. No one or a dozen other books influenced me nearly so much as these two. I copied out from Humboldt long passages about Teneriffe, and read them aloud on one of

he printed, for private circulation, an autobiographical sketch, *Chapters in my Life*, and subsequently some (undated) addenda. The well-known Soame Jenyns was cousin to Mr. Jenyns father.—F. D. Charles Darwin's suggested relationship is therefore wrong. Leonard Jenyns almost accepted the offer of the post on the *Beagle* before it was offered to Charles Darwin.—N. B.

the above-mentioned excursions, to (I think) Henslow, Ramsay and Dawes; for on a previous occasion I had talked about the glories of Teneriffe, and some of the party declared they would endeavour to go there; but I think that they were only half in earnest. I was, however, quite in earnest, and got an introduction to a merchant in London to enquire about ships; but the scheme was of course knocked on the head by the voyage of the *Beagle*.

My summer vacations were given up to collecting beetles, to some reading and short tours. In the autumn my whole time was devoted to shooting, chiefly at Woodhouse and Maer, and sometimes with young Eyton of Eyton.[42] Upon the whole the three years which I spent at Cambridge were the most joyful in my happy life; for I was then in excellent health, and almost always in high spirits.

As I had at first come up to Cambridge at Christmas, I was forced to keep two terms after passing my final examination, at the commencement of 1831; and Henslow then persuaded me to begin the study of geology. Therefore on my return to Shropshire I examined sections and coloured a map of parts round Shrewsbury. Professor Sedgwick intended to visit N. Wales in the beginning of August to pursue his famous geological investigation amongst the older rocks, and Henslow asked him to allow me to accompany him.[43] Accordingly he came and slept at my Father's house.

A short conversation with him during this evening produced a strong impression on my mind. Whilst examining an old gravel-pit near Shrewsbury a labourer told me that he had found in it a large worn tropical Volute shell, such as may be seen on the chimney-pieces of cottages; and as he would not sell the shell I was convinced that he had really found it in the pit. I told Sedgwick of

[42] Thomas Campbell Eyton, 1809–1880. Corresponded with Darwin and Agassiz, and opposed Darwinism.—N. B.
[43] In connection with this tour my father used to tell a story about Sedgwick: they had started from their inn one morning, and had walked a mile or two, when Sedgwick suddenly stopped, and vowed that he would return, being certain "that damned scoundrel" (the waiter) had not given the chambermaid the

the fact, and he at once said (no doubt truly) that it must have been thrown away by someone into the pit; but then added, if really embedded there it would be the greatest misfortune to geology, as it would overthrow all that we know about the superficial deposits of the midland counties. These gravel-beds belonged in fact to the glacial period, and in after years I found in them broken arctic shells. But I was then utterly astonished at Sedgwick not being delighted at so wonderful a fact as a tropical shell being found near the surface in the middle of England. Nothing before had ever made me thoroughly realise, though I had read various scientific books, that science consists in grouping facts so that general laws or conclusions may be drawn from them.

Next morning we started for Llangollen, Conway, Bangor, and Capel Curig. This tour was of decided use in teaching me a little how to make out the geology of a country. Sedgwick often sent me on a line parallel to his, telling me to bring back specimens of the rocks and to mark the stratification on a map. I have little doubt that he did this for my good, as I was too ignorant to have aided him. On this tour I had a striking instance how easy it is to overlook phenomena, however conspicuous, before they have been observed by anyone. We spent many hours in Cwm Idwal, examining all the rocks with extreme care, as Sedgwick was anxious to find fossils in them; but neither of us saw a trace of the wonderful glacial phenomena all around us; we did not notice the plainly scored rocks, the perched boulders, the lateral and terminal moraines. Yet these phenomena are so conspicuous that, as I declared in a paper published many years afterwards in the *Philosophical Magazine*,[44] a house burnt down by fire did not tell its story more plainly than did this valley. If it had still been filled by a glacier, the phenomena would have been less distinct than they now are.

---

sixpence entrusted to him for the purpose. He was ultimately persuaded to give up the project, seeing that there was no reason for suspecting the waiter of perfidy.—F. D.

[44] *Philosophical Magazine*, 1842.—F. D.

At Capel Curig I left Sedgwick and went in a straight line by compass and map across the mountains to Barmouth, never following any track unless it coincided with my course. I thus came on some strange wild places and enjoyed much this manner of travelling. I visited Barmouth to see some Cambridge friends who were reading there, and thence returned to Shrewsbury and to Maer for shooting; for at that time I should have thought myself mad to give up the first days of partridge-shooting for geology or any other science.

Voyage of the 'Beagle': from Dec. 27, 1831 to Oct. 2, 1836

ON RETURNING home from my short geological tour in N. Wales, I found a letter from Henslow, informing me that Captain Fitz-Roy[45] was willing to give up part of his own cabin to any young man who would volunteer to go with him without pay as naturalist to the Voyage of the Beagle. I have given as I believe in my MS. Journal an account of all the circumstances which then occurred; I will here only say that I was instantly eager to accept the offer, but my father strongly objected, adding the words fortunate for me,—"If you can find any man of common sense, who advises you to go, I will give my consent." So I wrote that evening and refused the offer. On the next morning I went to Maer to be ready for September 1st, and whilst out shooting, my uncle[46] sent

[45] Robert Fitz-Roy, 1805–1865. Vice-admiral, hydrographer and meteorologist. Son of Lord Charles Fitz-Roy, and grandson of the Duke of Grafton. Instituted systems of weather-warnings.—N. B.
[46] Josiah Wedgwood, son of Josiah Wedgwood the Potter.

for me, offering to drive me over to Shrewsbury and talk with my father. As my uncle thought it would be wise in me to accept the offer, and as my father always maintained that he was one of the most sensible men in the world, he at once consented in the kindest manner.[47] I had been rather extravagant at Cambridge and to console my father said, "that I should be deuced clever to spend more than my allowance whilst on board the *Beagle*"; but he answered with a smile, "But they all tell me you are very clever."

Next day I started for Cambridge to see Henslow, and thence to London to see Fitz-Roy, and all was soon arranged. Afterwards on becoming very intimate with Fitz-Roy, I heard that I had run a very narrow risk of being rejected, on account of the shape of my nose! He was an ardent disciple of Lavater, and was convinced that he could judge a man's character by the outline of his features; and he doubted whether anyone with my nose could possess sufficient energy and determination for the voyage. But I think he was afterwards well-satisfied that my nose had spoken falsely.

Fitz-Roy's character was a singular one, with many very noble features: he was devoted to his duty, generous to a fault, bold, determined, indomitably energetic, and an ardent friend to all under his sway. He would undertake any sort of trouble to assist those whom he thought deserved assistance. He was a handsome man, strikingly like a gentleman, with highly courteous manners, which resembled those of his maternal uncle, the famous Lord Castlereagh, as I was told by the Minister at Rio. Nevertheless he must have inherited much in his appearance from Charles II, for Dr. Wallich gave me a collection of photographs which he had made, and I was struck with the resemblance of one to Fitz-Roy;

[47] See Note 2, p. 190; letters from Charles Darwin and Josiah Wedgwood, refuting Dr. Robert's objections to the voyage. How Dr. Robert Darwin's objections to the Voyage were overcome.—N. B.

on looking at the name, I found it Ch. E. Sobieski Stuart, Count d'Albanie,[48] illegitimate descendant of the same monarch.

Fitz-Roy's temper was a most unfortunate one. This was shown not only by passion but by fits of long-continued moroseness against those who had offended him. His temper was usually worst in the early morning, and with his eagle eye he could generally detect something amiss about the ship, and was then unsparing in his blame. The junior officers when they relieved each other in the forenoon used to ask "whether much hot coffee had been served out this morning,—" which meant how was the Captain's temper? He was also somewhat suspicious and occasionally in very low spirits, on one occasion bordering on insanity. He seemed to me often to fail in sound judgment or common sense. He was extremely kind to me, but was a man very difficult to live with on the intimate terms which necessarily followed from our messing by ourselves in the same cabin. We had several quarrels; for when out of temper he was utterly unreasonable. For instance, early in the voyage at Bahia in Brazil he defended and praised slavery, which I abominated, and told me that he had just visited a great slave-owner, who had called up many of his slaves and asked them whether they were happy, and whether they wished to be free, and all answered "No." I then asked him, perhaps with a sneer, whether he thought that the answers of slaves in the presence of their master was worth anything. This made him excessively angry, and he said that as I doubted his word, we could not live any longer together. I thought that I should have been compelled to leave the ship; but as soon as the news spread, which it did quickly, as the captain sent for the first lieutenant to assuage his anger by abusing me, I was deeply gratified by receiving an invitation from all the gun-room officers to mess with them. But

[48] The Count d'Albanie's claim to Royal descent has been shown to be based on a myth. See the *Quarterly Review*, 1847, vol. lxxxi. p. 83; also Hayward's *Biographical and Critical Essays*, 1873, vol. ii. p. 201.—F. D.

after a few hours Fitz-Roy showed his usual magnanimity by sending an officer to me with an apology and a request that I would continue to live with him. I remember another instance of his candour. At Plymouth before we sailed, he was extremely angry with a dealer in crockery who refused to exchange some article purchased in his shop: the Captain asked the man the price of a very expensive set of china and said "I should have purchased this if you had not been so disobliging." As I knew that the cabin was amply stocked with crockery, I doubted whether he had any such intention; and I must have shown my doubts in my face, for I said not a word. After leaving the shop he looked at me, saying You do not believe what I have said, and I was forced to own that it was so. He was silent for a few minutes and then said You are right, and I acted wrongly in my anger at the blackguard.

At Conception in Chile, poor Fitz-Roy was sadly overworked and in very low spirits; he complained bitterly to me that he must give a great party to all the inhabitants of the place. I remonstrated and said that I could see no such necessity on his part under the circumstances. He then burst out into a fury, declaring that I was the sort of man who would receive any favours and make no return. I got up and left the cabin without saying a word, and returned to Conception where I was then lodging. After a few days I came back to the ship and was received by the Captain as cordially as ever, for the storm had by that time quite blown over. The first Lieutenant, however, said to me: "Confound you, philosopher, I wish you would not quarrel with the skipper; the day you left the ship I was dead-tired (the ship was refitting) and he kept me walking the deck till midnight abusing you all the time." The difficulty of living on good terms with a Captain of a Man-of-War is much increased by its being almost mutinous to answer him as one would answer anyone else; and by the awe in which he is held—or was held in my time, by all on board. I remember hearing a curious instance of this in the case of the purser of the *Adventure*,—the ship which sailed with the *Beagle* during the first voyage. The Purser was in a store in Rio de Janeiro, purchasing rum for the ship's company, and a little gentleman in plain clothes walked in. The Purser said to him, "Now Sir, be so kind as to taste this rum, and give me your opinion of it." The gentleman did as he was asked, and soon left the store. The store-keeper then asked the Purser, whether he knew that he had been speaking to the Captain of a Line of Battleships which had just come into the harbour. The poor Purser was struck dumb with horror; he let the glass of spirit drop from his hand onto the floor, and immediately went on board, and no persuasion, as an officer on the *Adventure* assured me, could make him go on shore again for fear of meeting the Captain after his dreadful act of familiarity.

I saw Fitz-Roy only occasionally after our return home, for I was always afraid of unintentionally offending him, and did so once, almost beyond mutual reconciliation. He was afterwards very indignant with me for having published so unorthodox a book (for he became very religious) as the *Origin of Species*. Towards the close of his life he was as I fear, much impoverished, and this was largely due to his generosity. Anyhow after his death a subscription was raised to pay his debts. His end was a melancholy one, namely suicide, exactly like that of his uncle Ld. Castlereagh, whom he resembled closely in manner and appearance.

His character was in several respects one of the most noble which I have ever known, though tarnished by grave blemishes.

The voyage of the *Beagle* has been by far the most important event in my life and has determined my whole career; yet it depended on so small a circumstance as my uncle offering to drive me 30 miles to Shrewsbury, which few uncles would have done, and on such a trifle as the shape of my nose. I have always felt that I owe to the voyage the first real training or education of my mind. I was led to attend closely to several branches of natural history, and thus my powers of observation were improved, though they were already fairly developed.

The investigation of the geology of all the places visited was far more important, as reasoning here comes into play. On first examining a new district nothing can appear more hopeless than the chaos of rocks; but by recording the stratification and nature of the rocks and fossils at many points, always reasoning and predicting what will be found elsewhere, light soon begins to dawn on the district, and the structure of the whole becomes more or less intelligible. I had brought with me the first volume of Lyell's *Principles of Geology*, which I studied attentively; and this book was of the highest service to me in many ways. The very first place which I examined, namely St. Jago in the Cape Verde islands, showed me clearly the wonderful superiority of Lyell's manner of treating geology, compared with that of any other author, whose works I had with me or ever afterwards read.[49]

Another of my occupations was collecting animals of all classes, briefly describing and roughly dissecting many of the marine ones; but from not being able to draw and from not having sufficient anatomical knowledge a great pile of MS. which I made during the voyage has proved almost useless. I thus lost much time, with the exception of that spent in acquiring some knowledge of the Crustaceans, as this was of service when in after years I undertook a monograph of the Cirripedia.

During some part of the day I wrote my Journal, and took much pains in describing carefully and vividly all that I had seen; and this was good practice. My Journal served, also, in part as letters to my home, and portions were sent to England, whenever there was an opportunity.

The above various special studies were, however, of no importance compared with the habit of energetic industry and of concentrated attention to whatever I was engaged in, which I then acquired. Everything about which I thought or read was made to

---

[49] The second volume of Lyell's *Principles of Geology* reached him in Monte Video in 1832.—N. B.

bear directly on what I had seen and was likely to see; and this habit of mind was continued during the five years of the voyage. I feel sure that it was this training which has enabled me to do whatever I have done in science.

Looking backwards, I can now perceive how my love for science gradually preponderated over every other taste. During the first two years my old passion for shooting survived in nearly full force, and I shot myself all the birds and animals for my collection; but gradually I gave up my gun more and more, and finally altogether to my servant, as shooting interfered with my work, more especially with making out the geological structure of a country. I discovered, though unconsciously and insensibly, that the pleasure of observing and reasoning was a much higher one than that of skill and sport. The primeval instincts of the barbarian slowly yielded to the acquired tastes of the civilised man. That my mind became developed through my pursuits during the voyage, is rendered probable by a remark made by my father, who was the most acute observer whom I ever saw, of a sceptical disposition, and far from being a believer in phrenology; for on first seeing me after the voyage, he turned round to my sisters and exclaimed, "Why, the shape of his head is quite altered."

To return to the voyage. On September 11th (1831) I paid a flying visit with Fitz-Roy to the *Beagle* at Plymouth. Thence to Shrewsbury to wish my father and sisters a long farewell. On Oct. 24th, I took up my residence at Plymouth, and remained there until December 27th when the *Beagle* finally left the shores of England for her circumnavigation of the world. We made two earlier attempts to sail, but were driven back each time by heavy gales. These two months at Plymouth were the most miserable which I ever spent, though I exerted myself in various ways. I was out of spirits at the thought of leaving all my family and friends for so long a time, and the weather seemed to me inexpressibly gloomy. I was also troubled with palpitations and pain about the heart, and like many a young ignorant man, especially one with a smattering of medical knowledge, was convinced that I had heart-disease. I did not consult any doctor, as I fully expected to hear the verdict that I was not fit for the voyage, and I was resolved to go at all hazards.

I need not here refer to the events of the voyage—where we went and what we did—as I have given a sufficiently full account in my published Journal. The glories of the vegetation of the Tropics rise before my mind at the present time more vividly than anything else. Though the sense of sublimity, which the great deserts of Patagonia and the forest-clad mountains of Tierra del Fuego excited in me, has left an indelible impression on my mind. The sight of a naked savage in his native land is an event which can never be forgotten. Many of my excursions on horseback through wild countries, or in the boats, some of which lasted several weeks, were deeply interesting; their discomfort and some degree of danger were at that time hardly a drawback and none at all afterwards. I also reflect with high satisfaction on some of my scientific work, such as solving the problem of coral-islands, and making out the geological structure of certain islands, for instance, St. Helena. Nor[50] must I pass over the discovery of the singular relations of the animals and plants inhabiting the several islands of the Galapagos archipelago, and of all of them to the inhabitants of South America.

As far as I can judge of myself I worked to the utmost during the voyage from the mere pleasure of investigation, and from my strong desire to add a few facts to the great mass of facts in natural science. But I was also ambitious to take a fair place among scientific men,—whether more ambitious or less so than most of my fellow-workers I can form no opinion.

The geology of St. Jago is very striking yet simple: a stream of lava formerly flowed over the bed of the sea, formed of triturated recent shells and corals, which it has baked into a hard white rock.

[50] Addendum to end of paragraph.—N. B.

Since then the whole island has been upheaved. But the line of white rock revealed to me a new and important fact, namely that there had been afterwards subsidence round the craters, which had since been in action, and had poured forth lava. It then first dawned on me that I might perhaps write a book on the geology of the various countries visited, and this made me thrill with delight. That was a memorable hour to me, and how distinctly I can call to mind the low cliff of lava beneath which I rested, with the sun glaring hot, a few strange desert plants growing near, and with living corals in the tidal pools at my feet. Later in the voyage Fitz-Roy asked to read some of my Journal, and declared it would be worth publishing; so here was a second book in prospect!

Towards the close of our voyage I received a letter whilst at Ascension, in which my sisters told me that Sedgwick had called on my father and said that I should take a place among the leading scientific men. I could not at the time understand how he could have learnt anything of my proceedings, but I heard (I believe afterwards) that Henslow had read some of the letters which I wrote to him before the Philosophical Soc. of Cambridge[51] and had printed them for private distribution. My collection of fossil bones, which had been sent to Henslow, also excited considerable attention amongst palæontologists. After reading this letter I clambered over the mountains of Ascension with a bounding step and made the volcanic rocks resound under my geological hammer! All this shows how ambitious I was; but I think that I can say with truth that in after years, though I cared in the highest degree for the approbation of such men as Lyell and Hooker, who were my friends, I did not care much about the general public. I do not mean to say that a favourable review or a large sale of my books did not please me greatly; but the pleasure was

[51] Read at the meeting held November 16, 1835, and printed in a pamphlet of 31 pp. for distribution among the members of the Society.—F. D.

a fleeting one, and I am sure that I have never turned one inch out of my course to gain fame.

From my return to England Oct. 2, 1836 to my marriage Jan. 29, 1839

THESE TWO years and three months were the most active ones which I ever spent, though I was occasionally unwell and so lost some time. After going backwards and forwards several times between Shrewsbury, Maer, Cambridge and London, I settled in lodgings at Cambridge[52] on December 13th, where all my collections were under the care of Henslow. I stayed here three months and got my minerals and rocks examined by the aid of Prof. Miller.[53]

I began preparing my Journal of travels, which was not hard work, as my MS. Journal had been written with care, and my chief labour was making an abstract of my more interesting scientific results. I sent also, at the request of Lyell, a short account of my observations on the elevation of the coast of Chile to the Geological Society.[54]

On March 7th, 1837, I took lodgings in Great Marlborough Street in London and remained there for nearly two years until I was married.[55] During these two years I finished my Journal, read several papers before the Geological Society, began preparing the

---

[52] In Fitzwilliam Street.—F. D.
[53] William Hallowes Miller, 1801–1880. Professor of Mineralogy, 1832–70.—N. B.
[54] Geolog. Soc. Proc. ii. 1838, pp. 446–449.—F. D.
[55] See Note 3, p. 194. "This is the Question."—N. B.

MS. for my *Geological Observations* and arranged for the publication of the *Zoology of the Voyage of the Beagle.* In July I opened my first note-book for facts in relation to the *Origin of Species,* about which I had long reflected, and never ceased working on for the next twenty years.

During these two years I also went a little into society, and acted as one of the hon. secretaries of the Geological Society. I saw a great deal of Lyell. One of his chief characteristics was his sympathy with the work of others; and I was as much astonished as delighted at the interest which he showed when on my return to England I explained to him my views on coral reefs. This encouraged me greatly, and his advice and example had much influence on me. During this time I saw also a good deal of Robert Brown[56] "facile princeps botanicorum." I used often to call and sit with him during his breakfast on Sunday mornings, and he poured forth a rich treasure of curious observations and acute remarks, but they almost always related to minute points, and he never with me discussed large and general questions in science.

During these two years I took several short excursions as a relaxation, and one longer one to the parallel roads of Glen Roy, an account of which was published in the *Philosophical Transactions.*[57] This paper was a great failure, and I am ashamed of it. Having been deeply impressed with what I had seen of the elevation of the land in S. America, I attributed the parallel lines to the action of the sea; but I had to give up this view when Agassiz propounded his glacier-lake theory. Because no other explanation was possible under our then state of knowledge, I argued in favour of sea-action; and my error has been a good lesson to me never to trust in science to the principle of exclusion.

As I was not able to work all day at science I read a good deal during these two years on various subjects, including some meta-

[56] Robert Brown, 1773–1858. Botanist, Librarian to Linnean Society.—N. B.
[57] 1839, pp. 39–82.—F. D.

physical books, but I was not at [all] well fitted for such studies. About this time I took much delight in Wordsworth's and Coleridge's poetry, and can boast that I read the *Excursion* twice through. Formerly Milton's *Paradise Lost* had been my chief favourite, and in my excursions during the voyage of the *Beagle*, when I could take only a single small volume, I always chose Milton.

Religious Belief

DURING THESE two years[58] I was led to think much about religion. Whilst on board the *Beagle* I was quite orthodox, and I remember being heartily laughed at by several of the officers (though themselves orthodox) for quoting the Bible as an unanswerable authority on some point of morality. I suppose it was the novelty of the argument that amused them. But I had gradually come, by this time, to see that the Old Testament from its manifestly false history of the world, with the Tower of Babel, the rainbow as a sign, etc., etc., and from its attributing to God the feelings of a revengeful tyrant, was no more to be trusted than the sacred books of the Hindoos, or the beliefs of any barbarian. The question then continually rose before my mind and would not be banished,—is it credible that if God were now to make a revelation to the Hindoos, would he permit it to be connected with the belief in Vishnu, Siva, &c., as Christianity is connected with the Old Testament. This appeared to me utterly incredible.

By further reflecting that the clearest evidence would be requisite to make any sane man believe in the miracles by which Chris-

[58] October 1836 to January 1839.—F. D.

tianity is supported,—that the more we know of the fixed laws of nature the more incredible do miracles become,—that the men at that time were ignorant and credulous to a degree almost incomprehensible by us,—that the Gospels cannot be proved to have been written simultaneously with the events,—that they differ in many important details, far too important as it seemed to me to be admitted as the usual inaccuracies of eye-witnesses;—by such reflections as these, which I give not as having the least novelty or value, but as they influenced me, I gradually came to disbelieve in Christianity as a divine revelation. The fact that many false religions have spread over large portions of the earth like wild-fire had some weight with me. Beautiful as is the morality of the New Testament, it can hardly be denied that its perfection depends in part on the interpretation which we now put on metaphors and allegories.

But I was very unwilling to give up my belief;—I feel sure of this for I can well remember often and often inventing daydreams of old letters between distinguished Romans and manuscripts being discovered at Pompeii or elsewhere which confirmed in the most striking manner all that was written in the Gospels. But I found it more and more difficult, with free scope given to my imagination, to invent evidence which would suffice to convince me. Thus disbelief crept over me at a very slow rate, but was at last complete. The rate was so slow that I felt no distress, and have never since doubted even for a single second that my conclusion was correct. I can indeed hardly see how anyone ought to wish Christianity to be true; for if so the plain language of the text seems to show that the men who do not believe, and this would include my Father, Brother and almost all my best friends, will be everlastingly punished.

And this is a damnable doctrine.[59]

---

[59] Mrs. Darwin annotated this passage (from "and have never since doubted" . . . to "damnable doctrine") in her own handwriting. She writes:—"I should dislike

Although I did not think much about the existence of a personal God until a considerably later period of my life, I will here give the vague conclusions to which I have been driven. The old argument of design in nature, as given by Paley, which formerly seemed to me so conclusive, fails, now that the law of natural selection has been discovered. We can no longer argue that, for instance, the beautiful hinge of a bivalve shell must have been made by an intelligent being, like the hinge of a door by man. There seems to be no more design in the variability of organic beings and in the action of natural selection, than in the course which the wind blows. Everything in nature is the result of fixed laws. But I have discussed this subject at the end of my book on the *Variation of Domestic Animals and Plants*,[60] and the argument there given has never, as far as I can see, been answered.

But passing over the endless beautiful adaptations which we everywhere meet with, it may be asked how can the generally beneficent arrangement of the world be accounted for? Some writers indeed are so much impressed with the amount of suffering in the world, that they doubt if we look to all sentient beings, whether there is more of misery or of happiness;—whether the

---

the passage in brackets to be published. It seems to me raw. Nothing can be said too severe upon the doctrine of everlasting punishment for disbelief—but very few now wd. call that 'Christianity,' (tho' the words are there.) There is the question of verbal inspiration comes in too. E. D." Oct. 1882. This was written six months after her husband's death, in a second copy of the Autobiography in Francis's handwriting. The passage was not published. See Introduction.—N. B.
[60] My father asks whether we are to believe that the forms are preordained of the broken fragments of rock which are fitted together by man to build his houses. If not, why should we believe that the variations of domestic animals or plants are preordained for the sake of the breeder? "But if we give up the principle in one case, . . . no shadow of reason can be assigned for the belief that variations alike in nature and the result of the same general laws, which have been the groundwork through natural selection of the formation of the most perfectly adapted animals in the world, man included, were intentionally and specially guided."—*Variations of Animals and Plants,* 1st Edit. vol. ii. p. 431.—F. D.

world as a whole is a good or a bad one. According to my judgment happiness decidedly prevails, though this would be very difficult to prove. If the truth of this conclusion be granted, it harmonises well with the effects which we might expect from natural selection. If all the individuals of any species were habitually to suffer to an extreme degree they would neglect to propagate their kind; but we have no reason to believe that this has ever or at least often occurred. Some other considerations, moreover, lead to the belief that all sentient beings have been formed so as to enjoy, as a general rule, happiness.

Every one who believes, as I do, that all the corporeal and mental organs (excepting those which are neither advantageous or disadvantageous to the possessor) of all beings have been developed through natural selection, or the survival of the fittest, together with use or habit,[61] will admit that these organs have been formed so that their possessors may compete successfully with other beings, and thus increase in number. Now an animal may be led to pursue that course of action which is the most beneficial to the species by suffering, such as pain, hunger, thirst, and fear,—or by pleasure, as in eating and drinking and in the propagation of the species, &c. or by both means combined, as in the search for food. But pain or suffering of any kind, if long continued, causes depression and lessens the power of action; yet is well adapted to make a creature guard itself against any great or sudden evil. Pleasurable sensations, on the other hand, may be long continued without any depressing effect; on the contrary they stimulate the whole system to increased action. Hence it has come to pass that most or all sentient beings have been developed in such a manner through natural selection, that pleasurable sensations serve as their habitual guides. We see this in the pleasure from exertion,

---

[61] "together with use or habit" added later. The many corrections and alterations in this sentence show his increasing preoccupation with the possibility of other forces at work besides Natural Selection. See p. 15—N. B.

even occasionally from great exertion of the body or mind,—in the pleasure of our daily meals, and especially in the pleasure derived from sociability and from loving our families. The sum of such pleasures as these, which are habitual or frequently recurrent, give, as I can hardly doubt, to most sentient beings an excess of happiness over misery, although many occasionally suffer much. Such suffering, is quite compatible with the belief in Natural Selection, which is not perfect in its action, but tends only to render each species as successful as possible in the battle for life with other species, in wonderfully complex and changing circumstances.

That there is much suffering in the world no one disputes. Some have attempted to explain this in reference to man by imagining that it serves for his moral improvement. But the number of men in the world is as nothing compared with that of all other sentient beings, and these often suffer greatly without any moral improvement. A being so powerful and so full of knowledge as a God who could create the universe, is to our finite minds omnipotent and omniscient, and it revolts our understanding to suppose that his benevolence is not unbounded, for what advantage can there be in the sufferings of millions of the lower animals throughout almost endless time? This very old argument from the existence of suffering against the existence of an intelligent first cause seems to me a strong one; whereas, as just remarked, the presence of much suffering agrees well with the view that all organic beings have been developed through variation and natural selection.

At the present day the most usual argument for the existence of an intelligent God is drawn from the deep inward conviction and feelings which are experienced by most persons. But it cannot be doubted that Hindoos, Mahomadans and others might argue in the same manner and with equal force in favour of the existence of one God, or of many Gods, or as with the Buddists of no God. There are also many barbarian tribes who cannot be said with any truth to believe in what we call God: they believe indeed in spirits or ghosts, and it can be explained, as Tyler and Herbert Spencer have shown, how such a belief would be likely to arise.

Formerly I was led by feelings such as those just referred to, (although I do not think that the religious sentiment was ever strongly developed in me), to the firm conviction of the existence of God, and of the immortality of the soul. In my Journal I wrote that whilst standing in the midst of the grandeur of a Brazilian forest, "it is not possible to give an adequate idea of the higher feelings of wonder, admiration, and devotion which fill and elevate the mind." I well remember my conviction that there is more in man than the mere breath of his body. But now the grandest scenes would not cause any such convictions and feelings to rise in my mind. It may be truly said that I am like a man who has become colour-blind, and the universal belief by men of the existence of redness makes my present loss of perception of not the least value as evidence. This argument would be a valid one if all men of all races had the same inward conviction of the existence of one God; but we know that this is very far from being the case. Therefore I cannot see that such inward convictions and feelings are of any weight as evidence of what really exists. The state of mind which grand scenes formerly excited in me, and which was intimately connected with a belief in God, did not essentially differ from that which is often called the sense of sublimity; and however difficult it may be to explain the genesis of this sense, it can hardly be advanced as an argument for the existence of God, any more than the powerful though vague and similar feelings excited by music.

With respect to immortality,[62] nothing shows me how strong and almost instinctive a belief it is, as the consideration of the view now held by most physicists, namely that the sun with all

[62] Addendum added later to end of paragraph.—N. B.

the planets will in time grow too cold for life, unless indeed some great body dashes into the sun and thus gives it fresh life.— Believing as I do that man in the distant future will be a far more perfect creature than he now is, it is an intolerable thought that he and all other sentient beings are doomed to complete annihilation after such long-continued slow progress. To those who fully admit the immortality of the human soul, the destruction of our world will not appear so dreadful.

Another source of conviction in the existence of God, connected with the reason and not with the feelings, impresses me as having much more weight. This follows from the extreme difficulty or rather impossibility of conceiving this immense and wonderful universe, including man with his capacity of looking far backwards and far into futurity, as the result of blind chance or necessity. When thus reflecting I feel compelled to look to a First Cause having an intelligent mind in some degree analogous to that of man; and I deserve to be called a Theist.

This conclusion[63] was strong in my mind about the time, as far as I can remember, when I wrote the *Origin of Species*; and it is since that time that it has very gradually with many fluctuations become weaker. But then arises the doubt—can the mind of man, which has, as I fully believe, been developed from a mind as low as that possessed by the lowest animal, be trusted when it draws such grand conclusions? May not these be the result of the connection between cause and effect which strikes us as a necessary one, but probably depends merely on inherited experience? Nor must we overlook the probability of the constant inculcation in a belief in God on the minds of children producing so strong and perhaps an inherited effect on their brains not yet fully developed, that it

[63] Addendum of four lines added later. In Charles's MS. copy the interleaved addition is in his eldest son's hand. In Francis's copy it is in Charles's own hand.—N. B.

would be as difficult for them to throw off their belief in God, as for a monkey to throw off its instinctive fear and hatred of a snake.[64]

I cannot pretend to throw the least light on such abstruse problems. The mystery of the beginning of all things is insoluble by us; and I for one must be content to remain an Agnostic.

A man who has no assured and ever present belief in the existence of a personal God or of a future existence with retribution and reward, can have for his rule of life, as far as I can see, only to follow those impulses and instincts which are the strongest or which seem to him the best ones. A dog acts in this manner, but he does so blindly. A man, on the other hand, looks forwards and backwards, and compares his various feelings, desires and recollections. He then finds, in accordance with the verdict of all the wisest men that the highest satisfaction is derived from following certain impulses, namely the social instincts. If he acts for the good of others, he will receive the approbation of his fellow men and gain the love of those with whom he lives; and this latter gain undoubtedly is the highest pleasure on this earth. By degrees it will become intolerable to him to obey his sensuous passions rather than his higher impulses, which when rendered habitual

---

[64] Added later. Emma Darwin wrote and asked Frank to omit this sentence when he was editing the Autobiography in 1885. The letter is as follows:—

"Emma Darwin to her son Francis. 1885.

My dear Frank,

There is one sentence in the Autobiography which I very much wish to omit, no doubt partly because your father's opinion that *all* morality has grown up by evolution is painful to me; but also because where this sentence comes in, it gives one a sort of shock—and would give an opening to say, however unjustly, that he considered all spiritual beliefs no higher than hereditary aversions or likings, such as the fear of monkeys towards snakes.

I think the disrespectful aspect would disappear if the first part of the conjecture was left without the illustration of the instance of monkeys and snakes. I don't think you need consult William about this omission, as it would not change the whole gist of the Autobiography. I should wish if possible to avoid giving pain to your father's religious friends who are deeply attached to him,

may be almost called instincts. His reason may occasionally tell him to act in opposition to the opinion of others, whose approbation he will then not receive; but he will still have the solid satisfaction of knowing that he has followed his innermost guide or conscience.—As for myself I believe that I have acted rightly in steadily following and devoting my life to science. I feel no remorse from having committed any great sin, but have often and often regretted that I have not done more direct good to my fellow creatures. My sole and poor excuse is much ill-health and my mental constitution, which makes it extremely difficult for me to turn from one subject or occupation to another. I can imagine with high satisfaction giving up my whole time to philanthropy, but not a portion of it; though this would have been a far better line of conduct.

Nothing[65] is more remarkable than the spread of scepticism or rationalism during the latter half of my life. Before I was engaged to be married, my father advised me to conceal carefully my doubts, for he said that he had known extreme misery thus caused with married persons. Things went on pretty well until the wife or husband became out of health, and then some women suffered miserably by doubting about the salvation of their husbands, thus making them likewise to suffer. My father added that he had known during his whole long life only three women who were scep-

---

and I picture to myself the way that sentence would strike them, even those so liberal as Ellen Tollett and Laura, much more Admiral Sullivan, Aunt Caroline, &c., and even the old servants.

Yours, dear Frank,

E. D."

This letter appeared in *Emma Darwin* by Henrietta Litchfield in the privately printed edition from the Cambridge University Press in 1904. In John Murray's public edition of 1915 it was omitted.—N. B.

[65] This paragraph has a note by Charles:—"Written in 1879—copied out Apl. 22, 1881." Probably refers also to previous paragraph.—N. B.

tics; and it should be remembered that he knew well a multitude of persons and possessed extraordinary power of winning confidence. When I asked him who the three women were, he had to own with respect to one of them, his sister-in-law Kitty Wedgwood, that he had no good evidence, only the vaguest hints, aided by the conviction that so clear-sighted a woman could not be a believer. At the present time, with my small acquaintance, I know (or have known) several married ladies, who believe very little more than their husbands. My father used to quote an unanswerable argument, by which an old lady, a Mrs. Barlow, who suspected him of unorthodoxy, hoped to convert him:—"Doctor, I know that sugar is sweet in my mouth, and I know that my Redeemer liveth."

From my marriage, Jan. 29, 1839, and residence
in Upper Gower Street to our leaving London
and settling at Down, Sep. 14, 1842

YOU ALL know well your Mother, and what a good Mother she has ever been to all of you. She has been my greatest blessing, and I can declare that in my whole life I have never heard her utter one word which I had rather have been unsaid. She has never failed in the kindest sympathy towards me, and has borne with the utmost patience my frequent complaints from ill-health and discomfort. I do not believe she has ever missed an opportunity of doing a kind action to anyone near her. I marvel at my good fortune that she, so infinitely my superior in every single moral quality, consented to be my wife. She has been my wise adviser and cheerful comforter throughout life, which without her would have been during a very long period a miserable one from ill-health. She has earned the love and admiration of every soul near her.[66]

(Mem: her beautiful letter to myself preserved, shortly after our marriage.)[67]

I have indeed been most happy in my family, and I must say to you my children that not one of you has ever given me one minute's anxiety, except on the score of health. There are, I suspect, very few fathers of five sons who could say this with entire truth. When you were very young it was my delight to play with you all, and I think with a sigh that such days can never return. From your earliest days to now that you are grown up, you have all, sons and daughters, ever been most pleasant, sympathetic and affectionate to us and to one another. When all or most of you are at home (as, thank Heavens, happens pretty frequently) no party can be, according to my taste, more agreeable, and I wish for no other society. We have suffered only one very severe grief in the death of Annie at Malvern on April 24th, 1851, when she was just over ten years old. She was a most sweet and affectionate child, and I feel sure would have grown into a delightful woman. But I need say nothing here of her character, as I wrote a short sketch of it shortly after her death. Tears still sometimes come into my eyes, when I think of her sweet ways.[68]

During the three years and eight months whilst we resided in London, I did less scientific work, though I worked as hard as I possibly could, than during any other equal length of time in my life. This was owing to frequently recurring unwellness and to one long and serious illness. The greater part of my time, when I could do anything, was devoted to my work on *Coral Reefs*, which I had begun before my marriage, and of which the last proof-sheet

[66] Included in *More Letters*, Vol I, p. 30, but not published in *Autobiography*.
[67] See Note 4, p. 197.
[68] The fuller account of Annie can be found in *Life and Letters*, Vol. I, p. 132.
—N. B.

was corrected on May 6th, 1842. This book, though a small one, cost me twenty months of hard work, as I had to read every work on the islands of the Pacific and to consult many charts. It was thought highly of by scientific men, and the theory therein given is, I think, now well established.

No other work of mine was begun in so deductive a spirit as this; for the whole theory was thought out on the west coast of S. America before I had seen a true coral reef. I had therefore only to verify and extend my views by a careful examination of living reefs. But it should be observed that I had during the two previous years been incessantly attending to the effects on the shores of S. America of the intermittent elevation of the land, together with denudation and the deposition of sediment. This necessarily led me to reflect much on the effects of subsidence, and it was easy to replace in imagination the continued deposition of sediment by the upward growth of coral. To do this was to form my theory of the formation of barrier-reefs and atolls.

Besides my work on coral-reefs, during my residence in London, I read before the Geological Society papers on the Erratic Boulders of S. America,[69] on Earthquakes,[70] and on the Formation by the Agency of Earth-worms of Mould.[71] I also continued to superintend the publication of the *Zoology of the Voyage of the Beagle*. Nor did I ever intermit collecting facts bearing on the origin of species; and I could sometimes do this when I could do nothing else from illness.

In the summer of 1842 I was stronger than I had been for some time and took a little tour by myself in N. Wales, for the sake of observing the effects of the old glaciers which formerly filled all the larger valleys. I published a short account of what I saw in the *Philosophical Magazine*.[72] This excursion interested me

---

[69] *Geolog. Soc. Proc. iii.* 1842.

[70] *Geolog. Trans. v.* 1840.

[71] *Geolog. Soc. Proc. ii.* 1838.—F. D.

[72] *Philosophical Magazine*, 1842.

greatly, and it was the last time I was ever strong enough to climb mountains or to take long walks, such as are necessary for geological work.

During the early part of our life in London,[73] I was strong enough to go into general society, and saw a good deal of several scientific men and other more or less distinguished men. I will give my impressions with respect to some of them, though I have little to say worth saying.

I saw more of Lyell than of any other man both before and after my marriage. His mind was characterised, as it appeared to me, by clearness, caution, sound judgment and a good deal of originality. When I made any remark to him on Geology, he never rested until he saw the whole case clearly and often made me see it more clearly than I had done before. He would advance all possible objections to my suggestion, and even after these were exhausted would long remain dubious. A second characteristic was his hearty sympathy with the work of other scientific men.

On my return from the voyage of the *Beagle*, I explained to him my views on coral-reefs, which differed from his, and I was greatly surprised and encouraged by the vivid interest which he showed. On such occasions, while absorbed in thought, he would throw himself into the strangest attitudes, often resting his head on the seat of a chair, while standing up. His delight in science was ardent, and he felt the keenest interest in the future progress of mankind. He was very kind-hearted, and thoroughly liberal in his religious beliefs or rather disbeliefs; but he was a strong theist. His candour was highly remarkable. He exhibited this by becoming a convert to the Descent-theory, though he had gained much fame by opposing Lamarck's views, and this after he had grown old. He reminded me that I had many years before said to him, when discussing the opposition of the old school of geolo-

[73] These reminiscences until "Residence at Down" (p. 94) added Apl. 1881, which accounts for the slight repetition.—N. B.

gists to his new views, "What a good thing it would be, if every scientific man was to die when sixty years old, as afterwards he would be sure to oppose all new doctrines." But he hoped that now he might be allowed to live. He had a strong sense of humour and often told amusing anecdotes. He was very fond of society, especially of eminent men, and of persons high in rank; and this over-estimation of a man's position in the world, seemed to me his chief foible. He used to discuss with Lady Lyell as a most serious question, whether or not they should accept some particular invitation. But as he would not dine out more than three times a week on account of the loss of time, he was justi-fied in weighing his invitations with some care. He looked for-ward to going out oftener in the evening with advancing years, as to a great reward; but the good time never came, as his strength failed.

The science of Geology is enormously indebted to Lyell—more so, as I believe, than to any other man who ever lived. When I was starting on the voyage of the *Beagle*, the sagacious Henslow, who, like all other geologists believed at that time in successive cata-clysms, advised me to get and study the first volume of the *Prin-ciples*, which had then just been published, but on no account to accept the views therein advocated. How differently would any one now speak of the *Principles*! I am proud to remember that the first place, namely St. Jago, in the Cape Verde Archipelago, which I geologised, convinced me of the infinite superiority of Lyell's views over those advocated in any other work known to me.

The powerful effects of Lyell's works could formerly be plainly seen in the different progress of the science in France and Eng-land. The present total oblivion of Elie de Beaumont's wild hypotheses, such as his *Craters of Elevation* and *Lines of Elevation* (which latter hypothesis I heard Sedgwick at the Geolog. Soc. lauding to the skies), may be largely attributed to Lyell.

All the leading geologists were more or less known by me, at the time when geology was advancing with triumphant steps. I liked most of them, with the exception of Buckland,[74] who though very good-humoured and good-natured seemed to me a vulgar and almost coarse man. He was incited more by a craving for notoriety, which sometimes made him act like a buffoon, than by a love of science. He was not, however, selfish in his desire for notoriety; for Lyell, when a very young man, consulted him about communicating a poor paper to the Geol. Soc. which had been sent him by a stranger, and Buckland answered—"You had better do so, for it will be headed, 'Communicated by Charles Lyell,' and thus your name will be brought before the public."

The services rendered to geology by Murchison[75] by his classification of the older formations cannot be over-estimated; but he was very far from possessing a philosophical mind. He was very kind-hearted and would exert himself to the utmost to oblige anyone. The degree to which he valued rank was ludicrous, and he displayed this feeling and his vanity with the simplicity of a child. He related with the utmost glee to a large circle, including many mere acquaintances, in the rooms of the Geolog. Soc. how the Czar Nicholas, when in London, had patted him on the shoulder and had said, alluding to his geological work—"Mon ami, Russia is grateful to you," and then Murchison added rubbing his hands together, "The best of it was that Prince Albert heard it all." He announced one day to the Council of the Geolog. Soc. that his great work on the Silurian system was at last published; and he then looked at all who were present and said, "You will every one of you find your name in the Index," as if this was the height of glory.

I saw a good deal of Robert Brown, "facile Princeps Botanicorum," as he was called by Humboldt; and before I was married I

<hr />

[74] William Buckland, 1784–1856, Geologist, professor of mineralogy at Oxford, 1813; President of Geological Society, 1824 and 1840.—N. B.
[75] Roderick Impey Murchison, 1792–1871. Studied secondary rocks. F.R.S. 1826. President R. Geog. Soc. 1843; received Russian Orders; knighted 1846; K.C.B., 1863; baronet, 1866.—N. B.

used to go and sit with him almost every Sunday morning. He seemed to me to be chiefly remarkable for the minuteness of his observations and their perfect accuracy. He never propounded to me any large scientific views in biology. His knowledge was extraordinarily great, and much died with him, owing to his excessive fear of ever making a mistake. He poured out his knowledge to me in the most unreserved manner, yet was strangely jealous on some points. I called on him two or three times before the voyage of the *Beagle*, and on one occasion he asked me to look through a microscope and describe what I saw. This I did, and believe now that it was the marvellous currents of protoplasm in some vegetable cell. I then asked him what I had seen; but he answered me, who was then hardly more than a boy and on the point of leaving England for five years, "That is my little secret." I suppose that he was afraid that I might steal his discovery. Hooker told me that he was a complete miser, and knew himself to be a miser, about his dried plants; and he would not lend specimens to Hooker, who was describing the plants of Tierra del Fuego, although well knowing that he himself would never make any use of the collections from this country. On the other hand he was capable of the most generous actions. When old, much out of health and quite unfit for any exertion, he daily visited (as Hooker told me) an old man-servant, who lived at a distance and whom he supported, and read aloud to him. This is enough to make up for any degree of scientific penuriousness or jealousy. He was rather given to sneering at anyone who wrote about what he did not fully understand: I remember praising Whewell's *History of the Inductive Sciences* to him, and he answered, "Yes, I suppose that he has read the prefaces of very many books."

I often saw Owen,[76] whilst living in London, and admired him greatly, but was never able to understand his character and never

[76] Richard Owen, 1804–1892. Anatomist; F.R.S. 1834. First Hunterian professor of comparative anatomy and physiology, 1836–56. Attacked *Origin* 1860 in *Ed. Rev.* K.C.B. 1884.—N. B.

became intimate with him. After the publication of the *Origin of Species* he became my bitter enemy, not owing to any quarrel between us, but as far as I could judge out of jealousy at its success. Poor dear Falconer,[77] who was a charming man, had a very bad opinion of him, being convinced that he was not only ambitious, very envious and arrogant, but untruthful and dishonest. His power of hatred was certainly unsurpassed. When in former days I used to defend Owen, Falconer often said, "You will find him out some day," and so it has proved.

At a somewhat later period I became very intimate with Hooker,[78] who has been one of my best friends throughout life. He is a delightfully pleasant companion and most kind-hearted. One can see at once that he is honourable to the back-bone. His intellect is very acute, and he has a great power of generalisation. He is the most untirable worker that I have ever seen, and will sit the whole day working with the microscope, and be in the evening as fresh and pleasant as ever. He is in all ways very impulsive and somewhat peppery in temper; but the clouds pass away almost immediately. He once sent me an almost savage letter from a cause which will appear ludicrously small to an outsider, viz. because I maintained for a time the silly notion that our coal-plants had lived in shallow water in the sea. His indignation was all the greater because he could not pretend that he should ever have suspected that the Mangrove (and a few other marine plants which I named) had lived in the sea, if they had been found only in a fossil state. On another occasion he was almost equally indignant because I rejected with scorn the notion that a continent had

[77] Hugh Falconer, 1808–1865. Palæontologist and botanist. Worked largely in India; appointed to British Museum 1844 to arrange Indian fossils.—N. B.
[78] Joseph Dalton Hooker, 1817–1911. Botanist and traveller, increased knowledge of geographical distribution, and supported the Darwin-Wallace theory of *Origin of Species*. F.R.S. 1847. Succeeded his father as Director of Kew Gardens, 1865. Wrote *Students' Flora of the British Isles* and other works. C.B. 1869; O.M. 1907, etc.—N. B.

formerly extended between Australia and S. America. I have known hardly any man more lovable than Hooker.

A little later I became intimate with Huxley. His mind is as quick as a flash of lightning and as sharp as a razor. He is the best talker whom I have known. He never writes and never says anything flat. From his conversation no one would suppose that he could cut up his opponents in so trenchant a manner as he can do and does do. He has been a most kind friend to me and would always take any trouble for me. He has been the mainstay in England of the principle of the gradual evolution of organic beings. Much splendid work as he has done in Zoology, he would have done far more, if his time had not been so largely consumed by official and literary work, and by his efforts to improve the education of the country. He would allow me to say anything to him: many years ago I thought that it was a pity that he attacked so many scientific men, although I believe that he was right in each particular case, and I said so to him. He denied the charge indignantly, and I answered that I was very glad to hear that I was mistaken. We had been talking about his well-deserved attacks on Owen, so I said after a time, "How well you have exposed Ehrenberg's blunders;" he agreed and added that it was necessary for science that such mistakes should be exposed. Again after a time, I added: "Poor Agassiz has fared ill under your hands." Again I added another name, and now his bright eyes flashed on me, and he burst out laughing, anathematising me in some manner. He is a splendid man and has worked well for the good of mankind.

I may here mention a few other eminent men whom I have occasionally seen, but I have little to say about them worth saying. I felt a high reverence for Sir J. Herschel,[79] and was delighted to dine with him at his charming house at the C. of Good Hope

[79] John Frederick William Herschel, 1792–1871, Astronomer. F.R.S. 1813. Wrote on astronomical subjects, and on Light, Natural Philosophy, etc. Master of Mint, 1850–55. Created Baronet, 1838.—N. B.

and afterwards at his London house. I saw him, also, on a few other occasions. He never talked much, but every word which he uttered was worth listening to. He was very shy and he often had a distressed expression. Lady Caroline Bell, at whose house I dined at the C. of Good Hope, admired Herschel much, but said that he always came into a room as if he knew that his hands were dirty, and that he knew that his wife knew that they were dirty.

I once met at breakfast at Sir R. Murchison's house, the illustrious Humboldt, who honoured me by expressing a wish to see me. I was a little disappointed with the great man, but my anticipations probably were too high. I can remember nothing distinctly about our interview, except that Humboldt was very cheerful and talked much.

I used to call pretty often on Babbage[80] and regularly attended his famous evening parties. He was always worth listening to, but he was a disappointed and discontented man; and his expression was often or generally morose. I do not believe that he was half as sullen as he pretended to be. One day he told me that he had invented a plan by which all fires could be effectively stopped, but added,—"I shan't publish it—damn them all, let all their houses be burnt." The all were the inhabitants of London. Another day he told me that he had seen a pump on a road-side in Italy, with a pious inscription on it to the effect that the owner had erected the pump for the love of God and his country, that the tired wayfarer might drink. This led Babbage to examine the pump closely and he soon discovered that every time that a wayfarer pumped some water for himself, he pumped a larger quantity into the owner's house. Babbage then added—"There is only one thing which I hate more than piety,

[80] Charles Babbage, 1792–1871. F.R.S. 1816. Helped to found Astronomical Society 1820, and Statistical Society 1834. Mathematical and mechanical; but his inventions often proved abortive.—N. B.

and that is patriotism." But I believe that his bark was much worse than his bite.

Herbert Spencer's conversation seemed to me very interesting, but I did not like him particularly, and did not feel that I could easily have become intimate with him. I think that he was extremely egotistical. After reading any of his books, I generally feel enthusiastic admiration for his transcendent talents, and have often wondered whether in the distant future he would rank with such great men as Descartes, Leibnitz, etc., about whom, however, I know very little. Nevertheless I am not conscious of having profited in my own work by Spencer's writings. His deductive manner of treating every subject is wholly opposed to my frame of mind. His conclusions never convince me: and over and over again I have said to myself, after reading one of his discussions,— "Here would be a fine subject for half-a-dozen years' work." His fundamental generalisations (which have been compared in importance by some persons with Newton's laws!)—which I daresay may be very valuable under a philosophical point of view, are of such a nature that they do not seem to me to be of any strictly scientific use. They partake more of the nature of definitions than of laws of nature. They do not aid one in predicting what will happen in any particular case. Anyhow they have not been of any use to me.

Speaking of H. Spencer reminds me of Buckle,[81] whom I once met at Hensleigh Wedgwood's. I was very glad to learn from him his system of collecting facts. He told me that he bought all the books which he read, and made a full index to each, of the facts which he thought might prove serviceable to him, and that he could always remember in what book he had read anything, for his memory was wonderful. I then asked him how at first he could judge what facts would be serviceable and he answered that he did not know, but that a sort of instinct guided him. From this habit

[81] Henry Thomas Buckle, 1821–1862. Self-educated historian.

of making indices, he was enabled to give the astonishing number of references on all sorts of subjects, which may be found in his *History of Civilisation*. This book I thought most interesting and read it twice; but I doubt whether his generalisations are worth anything. H. Spencer told me that he had never read a line of it! Buckle was a great talker, and I listened to him without saying hardly a word, nor indeed could I have done so, for he left no gaps. When Effie[82] began to sing, I jumped up and said that I must listen to her. This I suppose offended him, for after I had moved away, he turned round to a friend, and said (as was overheard by my brother), "Well Mr. Darwin's books are much better than his conversation." What he really meant was that I did not properly appreciate his conversation.

Of other great literary men, I once met Sydney Smith at Dean Milman's house. There was something inexplicably amusing in every word which he uttered. Perhaps this was partly due to the expectation of being amused. He was talking about Lady Cork, who was then extremely old. This was the lady, who, as he said, was once so much affected by one of his charity sermons, that she *borrowed* a guinea from a friend to put into the Plate. He now said, "It is generally believed that my dear old friend Lady Cork has been overlooked"; and he said this in such a manner that no one could for a moment doubt that he meant that his dear old friend had been overlooked by the devil. How he managed to express this I know not.

I likewise once met Macaulay at Lord Stanhope's (the historian's) house,[83] and as there was only one other man at dinner, I had a grand opportunity of hearing him converse, and he was very agreeable. He did not talk at all too much; nor indeed could such

---

[82] Euphemia Wedgwood, married T. H. Farrer in 1873 as second wife.—N. B.
[83] Philip Henry Stanhope, 1805–1875. Fifth Earl of Stanhope; historian, author, Conservative M.P.; under-secretary for Foreign Affairs; influential in forming National Portrait Gallery, etc.—N. B.

a man talk too much, as long as he allowed others to turn the stream of his conversation, and this he did allow.

Lord Stanhope once gave me a curious little proof of the accuracy and fulness of Macaulay's memory: many historians used often to meet at Lord Stanhope's house, and, in discussing various subjects, they would sometimes differ from Macaulay, and formerly they often referred to some book to see who was right; but latterly, as Lord Stanhope noticed, no historian ever took this trouble, and whatever Macaulay said was final.

On another occasion I met at Ld. Stanhope's house one of his parties of historians and other literary men, and amongst them were Motley[84] and Grote.[85] After luncheon I walked about Chevening Park for nearly an hour with Grote, and was much interested by his conversation and pleased by the simplicity and absence of all pretension in his manners.

I met another set of great men at breakfast at Ld. Stanhope's house in London. After breakfast was quite over, Monckton Milnes[86] (Ld. Houghton now) walked in, and after looking round, exclaimed—(justifying Sidney Smith's nickname of "the cool of the evening")—"Well, I declare, you are all very premature."

Long ago I dined occasionally with the old Earl Stanhope, the father of the historian. I have heard that his father, the democratic earl, well-known at the time of the French Revolution, had his son educated as a blacksmith, as he declared that every man ought to know some trade. The old Earl, whom I knew, was a strange

[84] John Lothrop Motley, 1814–1877. Born in Dorchester, Mass., but lived much in Europe, as the materials for his historical work were not available in U.S.A. Published *History of the Dutch Republic* in 1856.—N. B.

[85] George Grote, 1794–1871. Historian; an original founder of London University. F.R.S. 1857. Vice-Chancellor Lon. Univ. 1862.—N. B.

[86] Richard Monckton Milnes, 1809–1885. Intimate friend of Tennyson, Hallam and Thackeray. Conservative M.P. 1837; became a Liberal on Peel's conversion to Free Trade, and supported reforms. Created Baron Houghton 1863. Author of various works.—N. B.

man, but what little I saw of him, I liked much. He was frank, genial, and pleasant. He had strongly marked features, with a brown complexion, and his clothes, when I saw him, were all brown. He seemed to believe in everything which was to others utterly incredible. He said one day to me, "Why don't you give up your fiddle-faddle of geology and zoology, and turn to the occult sciences?" The historian (then Ld. Mahon) seemed shocked at such a speech to me, and his charming wife much amused.

The last man whom I will mention is Carlyle, seen by me several times at my brother's house and two or three times at my own house. His talk was very racy and interesting, just like his writings, but he sometimes went on too long on the same subject. I remember a funny dinner at my brother's, where, amongst a few others, were Babbage and Lyell, both of whom liked to talk. Carlyle, however, silenced every one by haranguing during the whole dinner on the advantages of silence. After dinner, Babbage, in his grimmest manner, thanked Carlyle for his very interesting Lecture on Silence.

Carlyle sneered at almost every one. One day in my house he called Grote's *History* "a fetid quagmire, with nothing spiritual about it." I always thought, until his *Reminiscences* appeared, that his sneers were partly jokes, but this now seems rather doubtful. His expression was that of a depressed, almost despondent, yet benevolent man; and it is notorious how heartily he laughed. I believe that his benevolence was real, though stained by not a little jealousy. No one can doubt about his extraordinary power of drawing vivid pictures of things and men—far more vivid, as it appears to me, than any drawn by Macaulay. Whether his pictures of men were true ones is another question.

He has been all-powerful in impressing some grand moral truths on the minds of men. On the other hand, his views about slavery were revolting. In his eyes might was right. His mind seemed to me a very narrow one; even if all branches of science, which he despised, are excluded. It is astonishing to me that

Kingsley should have spoken of him as a man well fitted to advance science. He laughed to scorn the idea that a mathematician, such as Whewell, could judge, as I maintained he could, of Goethe's views on light. He thought it a most ridiculous thing that any one should care whether a glacier moved a little quicker or a little slower, or moved at all. As far as I could judge, I never met a man with a mind so ill adapted for scientific research.

Whilst living in London, I attended as regularly as I could the meetings of several scientific societies, and acted as secretary to the Geological Society. But such attendance, and ordinary society, suited my health so badly that we resolved to live in the country, which we both preferred and have never repented of.[87]

Residence at Down, from Sep. 14, 1842, to the present time, 1876

AFTER SEVERAL fruitless searches in Surrey and elsewhere, we found this house and purchased it. I was pleased with the diversified appearance of the vegetation proper to a chalk district, and so unlike what I had been accustomed to in the Midland counties; and still more pleased with the extreme quietness and rusticity of the place. It is not, however, quite so retired a place as a writer in a German periodical makes it, who says that my house can be approached only by a mule-track! Our fixing ourselves here has answered admirably in one way which we did not anticipate, namely, by being very convenient for frequent visits from our children, who never miss an opportunity of doing so when they can.

Few persons can have lived a more retired life than we have

[87] End of reminiscences, Apl. 1881, beginning p. 83.—N. B.

done. Besides short visits to the houses of relations, and occasionally to the seaside or elsewhere, we have gone nowhere. During the first part of our residence we went a little into society, and received a few friends here; but my health almost always suffered from the excitement, violent shivering and vomiting attacks being thus brought on. I have therefore been compelled for many years to give up all dinner-parties; and this has been somewhat of a deprivation to me, as such parties always put me into high spirits. From the same cause I have been able to invite here very few scientific acquaintances. Whilst I was young and strong I was capable of very warm attachments, but of late years, though I still have very friendly feelings towards many persons, I have lost the power of becoming deeply attached to anyone, not even so deeply to my good and dear friends Hooker and Huxley, as I should formerly have been. As far as I can judge this grievous loss of feeling has gradually crept over me, from the expectation of much distress afterwards from exhaustion having become firmly associated in my mind with seeing and talking with anyone for an hour, except my wife and children.

My chief enjoyment and sole employment throughout life has been scientific work; and the excitement from such work makes me for the time forget, or drives quite away, my daily discomfort. I have therefore nothing to record during the rest of my life, except the publication of my several books. Perhaps a few details how they arose may be worth giving.

My Several Publications

IN THE early part of 1844, my observations on the Volcanic Islands visited during the voyage of the *Beagle* were published. In 1845, I took much pains in correcting a new edition of my *Jour-*

nal of Researches, which was originally published in 1839 as part of
Fitz-Roy's work. The success of this my first literary child always
tickles my vanity more than that of any of my other books. Even
to this day it sells steadily in England and the United States, and
has been translated for the second time into German, and into
French and other languages. This success of a book of travels, especially of a scientific one, so many years after its first publication, is
surprising. Ten thousand copies have now been sold in England of
the second edition. In 1846 my *Geological Observations on South
America* were published. I record in a little diary, which I have
always kept, that my three geological books (*Coral Reefs* included)
consumed four and a half years' steady work; "and now it is ten
years since my return to England. How much time have I lost by
illness?" I have nothing to say about these three books except that
to my surprise new editions have lately been called for.[88]

In October 1846, I began to work on Cirripedia.[89] When on
the coast of Chile, I found a most curious form, which burrowed
into the shells of Concholepas, and which differed so much from
all other Cirripedes that I had to form a new sub-order for its sole
reception. Lately an allied burrowing genus has been found on the
shores of Portugal. To understand the structure of my new Cirri-
pede I had to examine and dissect many of the common forms:
and this gradually led me on to take up the whole group. I
worked steadily on the subject for the next eight years, and ultimately published two thick volumes,[90] describing all the known
living species, and two thin quartos on the extinct species. I do
not doubt that Sir E. Lytton Bulwer had me in his mind when he
introduces in one of his novels a Professor Long, who had written
two huge volumes on Limpets.

Although I was employed during eight years on this work, yet

[88] *Geological Observations*, 2nd Edit. 1876. *Coral Reefs*, 2nd Edit. 1874.—F. D.
[89] Barnacles.—N. B.
[90] Published by the Ray Society.—F. D.

I record in my diary that about two years out of this time was lost by illness. On this account I went in 1848 for some months to Malvern for hydropathic treatment, which did me much good, so that on my return home I was able to resume work. So much was I out of health that when my dear father died on November 13th, 1847,[91] I was unable to attend his funeral or to act as one of his executors.

My work on the Cirripedia possesses, I think, considerable value, as besides describing several new and remarkable forms, I made out the homologies of the various parts—I discovered the cementing apparatus, though I blundered dreadfully about the cement glands—and lastly I proved the existence in certain genera of minute males complemental to and parasitic on the hermaphrodites. This latter discovery has at last been fully confirmed; though at one time a German writer was pleased to attribute the whole account to my fertile imagination. The Cirripedes form a highly varying and difficult group of species to class; and my work was of considerable use to me, when I had to discuss in the *Origin of Species* the principles of a natural classification. Nevertheless, I doubt whether the work was worth the consumption of so much time.

From September 1854 onwards I devoted all my time to arranging my huge pile of notes, to observing, and experimenting, in relation to the transmutation of species. During the voyage of the *Beagle* I had been deeply impressed by discovering in the Pampean formation great fossil animals covered with armour like that on the existing armadillos; secondly, by the manner in which closely allied animals replace one another in proceeding southwards over the Continent; and thirdly, by the South American character of most of the productions of the Galapagos archipelago, and more especially by the manner in which they differ

[91] The date of Dr. Robert's death is given as 1848 in *Life and Letters*. In the MS. the date is clearly written 1847—a curious error.—N. B.

slightly on each island of the group; none of these islands appearing to be very ancient in a geological sense.

It was evident that such facts as these, as well as many others, could be explained on the supposition that species gradually become modified; and the subject haunted me. But it was equally evident that neither the action of the surrounding conditions, nor the will of the organisms (especially in the case of plants), could account for the innumerable cases in which organisms of every kind are beautifully adapted to their habits of life,—for instance, a woodpecker or tree-frog to climb trees, or a seed for dispersal by hooks or plumes. I had always been much struck by such adaptations, and until these could be explained it seemed to me almost useless to endeavour to prove by indirect evidence that species have been modified.

After my return to England it appeared to me that by following the example of Lyell in Geology, and by collecting all facts which bore in any way on the variation of animals and plants under domestication and nature, some light might perhaps be thrown on the whole subject. My first note-book was opened in July 1837. I worked on true Baconian principles, and without any theory collected facts on a wholesale scale, more especially with respect to domesticated productions, by printed enquiries, by conversation with skilful breeders and gardeners, and by extensive reading. When I see the list of books of all kinds which I read and abstracted, including whole series of Journals and Transactions, I am surprised at my industry. I soon perceived that selection was the keystone of man's success in making useful races of animals and plants. But how selection could be applied to organisms living in a state of nature remained for some time a mystery to me.

In October 1838, that is, fifteen months after I had begun my systematic enquiry, I happened to read for amusement Malthus on *Population*, and being well prepared to appreciate the struggle for existence which everywhere goes on from long-continued observation of the habits of animals and plants, it at once struck me that under these circumstances favourable variations would tend to be preserved, and unfavourable ones to be destroyed. The result of this would be the formation of new species. Here, then, I had at last got a theory by which to work; but I was so anxious to avoid prejudice, that I determined not for some time to write even the briefest sketch of it. In June 1842 I first allowed myself the satisfaction of writing a very brief abstract of my theory in pencil in 35 pages; and this was enlarged during the summer of 1844 into one of 230 pages, which I had fairly copied out and still possess.

But at that time I overlooked one problem of great importance; and it is astonishing to me, except on the principle of Columbus and his egg, how I could have overlooked it and its solution. This problem is the tendency in organic beings descended from the same stock to diverge in character as they become modified. That they have diverged greatly is obvious from the manner in which species of all kinds can be classed under genera, genera under families, families under sub-orders, and so forth; and I can remember the very spot in the road, whilst in my carriage, when to my joy the solution occurred to me; and this was long after I had come to Down. The solution, as I believe, is that the modified offspring of all dominant and increasing forms tend to become adapted to many and highly diversified places in the economy of nature.

Early in 1856 Lyell advised me to write out my views pretty fully, and I began at once to do so on a scale three or four times as extensive as that which was afterwards followed in my *Origin of Species*; yet it was only an abstract of the materials which I had collected, and I got through about half the work on this scale. But my plans were overthrown, for early in the summer of 1858 Mr. Wallace,[92] who was then in the Malay archipelago, sent me an

[92] Alfred Russell Wallace, 1823–1913, naturalist and traveller, author of various works on geographical distribution and evolution. F.R.S. 1893.—N. B.

essay *On the Tendency of Varieties to depart indefinitely from the Original Type*; and this essay contained exactly the same theory as mine. Mr. Wallace expressed the wish that if I thought well of his essay, I should send it to Lyell for perusal.

The circumstances under which I consented at the request of Lyell and Hooker to allow of an extract from my MS., together with a letter to Asa Gray, dated September 5, 1857, to be published at the same time with Wallace's Essay, are given in the *Journal of the Proceedings of the Linnean Society*, 1858, p. 45. I was at first very unwilling to consent, as I thought Mr. Wallace might consider my doing so unjustifiable, for I did not then know how generous and noble was his disposition. The extract from my MS. and the letter to Asa Gray had neither been intended for publication, and were badly written. Mr. Wallace's essay, on the other hand, was admirably expressed and quite clear. Nevertheless, our joint productions excited very little attention, and the only published notice of them which I can remember was by Professor Haughton of Dublin, whose verdict was that all that was new in them was false, and what was true was old. This shows how necessary it is that any new view should be explained at considerable length in order to arouse public attention.

In September 1858 I set to work by the strong advice of Lyell and Hooker to prepare a volume on the transmutation of species, but was often interrupted by ill-health, and short visits to Dr. Lane's delightful hydropathic establishment at Moor Park. I abstracted the MS. begun on a much larger scale in 1856, and completed the volume on the same reduced scale. It cost me thirteen months and ten days' hard labour. It was published under the title of the *Origin of Species*, in November 1859. Though considerably added to and corrected in the later editions, it has remained substantially the same book.

It is no doubt the chief work of my life. It was from the first highly successful. The first small edition of 1250 copies was sold on the day of publication, and a second edition of 3000 copies soon afterwards. Sixteen thousand copies have now (1876) been sold in England and considering how stiff a book it is, this is a large sale. It has been translated into almost every European tongue, even into such languages as Spanish, Bohemian, Polish, and Russian. It has also, according to Miss Bird, been translated into Japanese, and is there much studied.[93] Even an essay in Hebrew has appeared on it, showing that the theory is contained in the Old Testament! The reviews were very numerous; for a time I collected all that appeared on the *Origin* and on my related books, and these amount (excluding newspaper reviews) to 265; but after a time I gave up the attempt in despair. Many separate essays and books on the subject have appeared; and in Germany a catalogue or bibliography on "Darwinismus" has appeared every year or two.

The success of the *Origin* may, I think, be attributed in large part to my having long before written two condensed sketches, and to my having finally abstracted a much larger manuscript, which was itself an abstract. By this means I was enabled to select the more striking facts and conclusions. I had, also, during many years, followed a golden rule, namely, that whenever a published fact, a new observation or thought came across me, which was opposed to my general results, to make a memorandum of it without fail and at once; for I had found by experience that such facts and thoughts were far more apt to escape from the memory than favourable ones. Owing to this habit, very few objections were raised against my views which I had not at least noticed and attempted to answer.

It has sometimes been said that the success of the *Origin* proved "that the subject was in the air," or "that men's minds were prepared for it." I do not think that this is strictly true, for I occasionally sounded not a few naturalists, and never happened to come across a single one who seemed to doubt about the per-

---

[93] Miss Bird is mistaken, as I learn from Professor Mitsukuri.—F. D.

manence of species. Even Lyell and Hooker, though they would listen with interest to me, never seemed to agree. I tried once or twice to explain to able men what I meant by natural selection, but signally failed. What I believe was strictly true is that innumerable well-observed facts were stored in the minds of naturalists, ready to take their proper places as soon as any theory which would receive them was sufficiently explained.[94] Another element in the success of the book was its moderate size; and this I owe to the appearance of Mr. Wallace's essay; had I published on the scale in which I began to write in 1856, the book would have been four or five times as large as the *Origin*, and very few would have had the patience to read it.

I gained much by my delay in publishing from about 1839, when the theory was clearly conceived, to 1859; and I lost nothing by it, for I cared very little whether men attributed most originality to me or Wallace; and his essay no doubt aided in the reception of the theory. I was forestalled in only one important point, which my vanity has always made me regret, namely, the explanation by means of the Glacial period of the presence of the same species of plants and of some few animals on distant mountain summits and in the arctic regions. This view pleased me so much that I wrote it out *in extenso*, and it was read by Hooker some years before E. Forbes published his celebrated memoir on the subject.[95] In the very few points in which we differed, I still think that I was in the right. I have never, of course, alluded in print to my having independently worked out this view.

Hardly any point gave me so much satisfaction when I was at work on the *Origin*, as the explanation of the wide difference in many classes between the embryo and the adult animal, and of the close resemblance of the embryos within the same class. No notice

---

[94] See Appendix, Part 1, on Charles and Erasmus Darwin, p. 121. Charles's doubts as to whether "the subject was in the air" are there discussed.—N. B.
[95] *Geol. Survey Mem.*, 1846.—F. D.

of this point was taken, as far as I remember, in the early reviews of the *Origin*, and I recollect expressing my surprise on this head in a letter to Asa Gray. Within late years several reviewers have given the whole credit of the idea to Fritz Müller and Häckel, who undoubtedly have worked it out much more fully, and in some respects more correctly than I did. I had materials for a whole chapter on the subject, and I ought to have made the discussion longer; for it is clear that I failed to impress my readers; and he who succeeds in doing so deserves, in my opinion, all the credit.

This leads me to remark that I have almost always been treated honestly by my reviewers, passing over those without scientific knowledge as not worthy of notice. My views have often been grossly misrepresented, bitterly opposed and ridiculed, but this has been generally done, as I believe, in good faith. I must, however, except Mr. Mivart,[96] who as an American expressed it in a letter has acted towards me "like a pettifogger," or as Huxley has said "like an Old Bailey lawyer." On the whole I do not doubt that my works have been over and over again greatly overpraised. I rejoice that I have avoided controversies, and this I owe to Lyell, who many years ago, in reference to my geological works, strongly advised me never to get entangled in a controversy, as it rarely did any good and caused a miserable loss of time and temper.

Whenever[97] I have found out that I have blundered, or that my work has been imperfect, and when I have been contemptuously criticised, and even when I have been overpraised, so that I have felt mortified, it has been my greatest comfort to say hundreds of times to myself that "I have worked as hard and as well as I could, and no man can do more than this." I remember when in Good

---

[96] St. George Jackson Mivart, 1827–1900, biologist. Became a Roman Catholic, but later repudiated ecclesiastical authority. An evolutionist, but an opponent of Charles Darwin. F.R.S. 1869.—N. B.

[97] This paragraph added, probably in 1881.—N. B.

Success Bay, in Tierra del Fuego, thinking, (and I believe that I wrote home to the effect) that I could not employ my life better than in adding a little to natural science. This I have done to the best of my abilities, and critics may say what they like, but they cannot destroy this conviction.

During the two last months of the year 1859 I was fully occupied in preparing a second edition of the *Origin*, and by an enormous correspondence. On January 7th, 1860, I began arranging my notes for my work on the *Variation of Animals and Plants under Domestication*; but it was not published until the beginning of 1868; the delay having been caused partly by frequent illnesses, one of which lasted seven months, and partly by having been tempted to publish on other subjects which at the time interested me more.

On May 15th, 1862, my little book on the *Fertilisation of Orchids*, which cost me ten months' work, was published: most of the facts had been slowly accumulated during several previous years. During the summer of 1839, and, I believe, during the previous summer, I was led to attend to the cross-fertilisation of flowers by the aid of insects, from having come to the conclusion in my speculations on the origin of species, that crossing played an important part in keeping specific forms constant. I attended to the subject more or less during every subsequent summer; and my interest in it was greatly enhanced by having procured and read in November 1841, through the advice of Robert Brown, a copy of C. K. Sprengel's[98] wonderful book, *Das entdeckte Geheimnis der Natur*. For some years before 1862 I had specially attended to the fertilisation of our British orchids; and it seemed to me the best plan to prepare as complete a treatise on this group of plants as well as I could, rather than to utilise the great mass of matter which I had slowly collected with respect to other plants.

---

[98] Christian Konrad Sprengel, 1750–1816. Schoolmaster at Spandau.—N. B.

My resolve proved a wise one; for since the appearance of my book, a surprising number of papers and separate works on the fertilisation of all kinds of flowers have appeared; and these are far better done than I could possibly have effected. The merits of poor old Sprengel, so long overlooked, are now fully recognised many years after his death.

During this same year I published in the *Journal of the Linnean Society*, a paper *On the Two Forms, or Dimorphic Condition of Primula*, and during the next five years, five other papers on dimorphic and trimorphic plants. I do not think anything in my scientific life has given me so much satisfaction as making out the meaning of the structure of these plants. I had noticed in 1838 or 1839 the dimorphism of *Linum flavum*, and had at first thought that it was merely a case of unmeaning variability. But on examining the common species of Primula, I found that the two forms were much too regular and constant to be thus viewed. I therefore became almost convinced that the common cowslip and primrose were on the high-road to become dioecious;—that the short pistil in the one form, and the short stamens in the other form were tending towards abortion. The plants were therefore subjected under this point of view to trial; but as soon as the flowers with short pistils fertilised with pollen from the short stamens, were found to yield more seeds than any other of the four possible unions, the abortion-theory was knocked on the head. After some additional experiment, it became evident that the two forms, though both were perfect hermaphrodites, bore almost the same relation to one another as do the two sexes of an ordinary animal. With Lythrum we have the still more wonderful case of three forms standing in a similar relation to one another. I afterwards found that the offspring from the union of two plants belonging to the same forms presented a close and curious analogy with hybrids from the union of two distinct species.

In the autumn of 1864 I finished a long paper on *Climbing Plants*, and sent it to the Linnean Society. The writing of this paper cost me four months: but I was so unwell when I received the proof-sheets that I was forced to leave them very badly and often obscurely expressed. The paper was little noticed, but when in 1875 it was corrected and published as a separate book it sold well. I was led to take up this subject by reading a short paper by Asa Gray, published in 1858, on the movements of the tendrils of a Cucurbitacean plant. He sent me seeds, and on raising some plants I was so much fascinated and perplexed by the revolving movements of the tendrils and stems, which movements are really very simple, though appearing at first very complex, that I procured various other kinds of Climbing Plants, and studied the whole subject. I was all the more attracted to it, from not being at all satisfied with the explanation which Henslow gave us in his Lectures, about Twining plants, namely, that they had a natural tendency to grow up in a spire. This explanation proved quite erroneous. Some of the adaptations displayed by climbing plants are as beautiful as those by Orchids for ensuring cross-fertilisation.

My *Variation of Animals and Plants under Domestication* was begun, as already stated, in the beginning of 1860, but was not published until the beginning of 1868. It is a big book, and cost me four years and two months' hard labour. It gives all my observations and an immense number of facts collected from various sources, about our domestic productions. In the second volume the causes and laws of variation, inheritance, &c., are discussed, as far as our present state of knowledge permits. Towards the end of the work I give my well-abused hypothesis of Pangenesis. An unverified hypothesis is of little or no value. But if any one should hereafter be led to make observations by which some such hypothesis could be established, I shall have done good service, as an astonishing number of isolated facts can thus be connected together and rendered intelligible. In 1875 a second and largely corrected edition, which cost me a good deal of labour, was brought out.

My *Descent of Man* was published in Feb. 1871. As soon as I had become, in the year 1837 or 1838, convinced that species were mutable productions, I could not avoid the belief that man must come under the same law. Accordingly I collected notes on the subject for my own satisfaction, and not for a long time with any intention of publishing. Although in the *Origin of Species*, the derivation of any particular species is never discussed, yet I thought it best, in order that no honourable man should accuse me of concealing my views, to add that by the work in question "light would be thrown on the origin of man and his history." It would have been useless and injurious to the success of the book to have paraded without giving any evidence my conviction with respect to his origin.

But when I found that many naturalists fully accepted the doctrine of the evolution of species, it seemed to me advisable to work up such notes as I possessed and to publish a special treatise on the origin of man. I was the more glad to do so, as it gave me an opportunity of fully discussing sexual selection,—a subject which had always greatly interested me. This subject, and that of the variation of our domestic productions, together with the causes and laws of variation, inheritance, etc., and the intercrossing of Plants, are the sole subjects which I have been able to write about in full, so as to use all the materials which I had collected. The *Descent of Man* took me three years to write, but then as usual some of this time was lost by ill-health, and some was consumed by preparing new editions and other minor works. A second and largely corrected edition of the *Descent* appeared in 1874.

My book on the *Expression of the Emotions in Men and Animals* was published in the autumn of 1872. I had intended to give only a chapter on the subject in the *Descent of Man*, but as soon as I began to put my notes together, I saw that it would require a separate Treatise.

My first child was born on December 27th, 1839, and I at once commenced to make notes on the first dawn of the various expressions which he exhibited, for I felt convinced, even at this early period, that the most complex and fine shades of expression must all have had a gradual and natural origin. During the summer of the following year, 1840, I read Sir C. Bell's[99] admirable work on Expression, and this greatly increased the interest which I felt in the subject, though I could not at all agree with his belief that various muscles had been specially created for the sake of expression. From this time forward I occasionally attended to the subject, both with respect to man and our domesticated animals. My book sold largely; 5267 copies having been disposed of on the day of publication.

In the summer of 1860 I was idling and resting near Hartfield, where two species of Drosera abound; and I noticed that numerous insects had been entrapped by the leaves. I carried home some plants, and on giving them insects saw the movements of the tentacles, and this made me think it probable that the insects were caught for some special purpose. Fortunately a crucial test occurred to me, that of placing a large number of leaves in various nitrogenous and non-nitrogenous fluids of equal density; and as soon as I found that the former alone excited energetic movements, it was obvious that here was a fine new field for investigation.

During subsequent years, whenever I had leisure, I pursued my experiments, and my book on *Insectivorous Plants* was published July 1875,—that is sixteen years after my first observations. The delay in this case, as with all my other books, has been a great advantage to me; for a man after a long interval can criticise his own work, almost as well as if it were that of another person. The fact that a plant should secrete, when properly excited, a fluid containing an acid and ferment, closely analogous to the digestive fluid of an animal, was certainly a remarkable discovery.

[99] Charles Bell, 1774–1842. Educated Edinburgh, F.C.S. Ed. 1799. Prof. of Surgery, Ed. 1847. Knighted; R.S. medallist 1829; wrote on the nervous system and Anatomy of Expression, etc.—N. B.

During this autumn of 1876 I shall publish on the *Effects of Cross- and Self-Fertilisation in the Vegetable Kingdom.* This book will form a complement to that on the *Fertilisation of Orchids,* in which I showed how perfect were the means for cross-fertilisation, and here I shall show how important are the results. I was led to make, during eleven years, the numerous experiments recorded in this volume, by a mere accidental observation; and indeed it required the accident to be repeated before my attention was thoroughly aroused to the remarkable fact that seedlings of self-fertilised parentage are inferior, even in the first generation, in height and vigour to seedlings of cross-fertilised parentage. I hope also to republish a revised edition of my book on Orchids, and hereafter my papers on dimorphic and trimorphic plants, together with some additional observations on allied points which I never have had time to arrange. My strength will then probably be exhausted, and I shall be ready to exclaim "Nunc dimittis."

The Effects of Cross- and Self-Fertilisation[100] was published in the autumn of 1876; and the results there arrived at explain, as I believe, the endless and wonderful contrivances for the transportal of pollen from one plant to another of the same species. I now believe, however, chiefly from the observations of Hermann Müller, that I ought to have insisted more strongly than I did on the many adaptations for self-fertilisation; though I was well aware of many such adaptations. A much enlarged edition of my *Fertilisation of Orchids* was published in 1877.

In this same year *The Different Forms of Flowers, etc.,* appeared, and in 1880 a second edition. This book consists chiefly of the several papers on heterostyled flowers, originally published by the Linnean Society, corrected, with much new matter added, together with observations on some other cases in which the same plant bears two kinds of flowers. As before remarked, no little dis-

[100] This long addendum added May 1st, 1881, to . . . "old geological thoughts.", p. 111.—N. B.

covery of mine ever gave me so much pleasure as the making out the meaning of heterostyled flowers. The results of crossing such flowers in an illegitimate manner, I believe to be very important as bearing on the sterility of hybrids; although these results have been noticed by only a few persons.

In 1879, I had a translation of Dr. Ernst Krause's *Life of Erasmus Darwin* published, and I added a sketch of his character and habits from materials in my possession. Many persons have been much interested by this little life, and I am surprised that only 800 or 900 copies were sold. Owing to my having accidentally omitted to mention that Dr. Krause had enlarged and corrected his article in German before it was translated, Mr. Samuel Butler abused me with almost insane virulence. How I offended him so bitterly, I have never been able to understand. The subject gave rise to some controversy in the Athenæum newspaper and Nature. I laid all the documents before some good judges, viz. Huxley, Leslie Stephen, Litchfield,[101] etc., and they were all unanimous that the attack was so baseless that it did not deserve any public answer; for I had already expressed privately my regret to Mr. Butler for my accidental omission. Huxley consoled me by quoting some German lines from Goethe, who had been attacked by someone, to the effect "that every Whale has its Louse."[102]

In 1880 I published, with Frank's assistance, our *Power of Movement in Plants.* This was a tough piece of work. The book bears somewhat the same relation to my little book on *Climbing Plants,* which *Cross-Fertilisation* did to the *Fertilisation of Orchids*; for in accordance with the principles of evolution it was impossible to account for climbing plants having been developed in so many widely different groups, unless all kinds of plants possess some slight power of movement of an analogous kind. This I

---

[101] His son-in-law, R. B. Litchfield.—N. B.
[102] See Appendix. Part 2. p. 135. On the Darwin-Butler controversy, with unpublished documents, including Huxley's letter in its entirety.—N. B.

proved to be the case, and I was further led to a rather wide generalisation, viz., that the great and important classes of movements, excited by light, the attraction of gravity, &c., are all modified forms of the fundamental movement of circumnutation. It has always pleased me to exalt plants in the scale of organised beings; and I therefore felt an especial pleasure in showing how many and what admirably well adapted movements the tip of a root possesses.

I have now (May 1, 1881) sent to the printers the MS. of a little book on *The Formation of Vegetable Mould through the Action of Worms.* This is a subject of but small importance; and I know not whether it will interest any readers,[103] but it has interested me. It is the completion of a short paper read before the Geological Society more than forty years ago, and has revived old geological thoughts.[104]

I have now mentioned all the books which I have published, and these have been the milestones in my life, so that little remains to be said. I am not conscious of any change in my mind during the last thirty years, excepting in one point presently to be mentioned; nor indeed could any change have been expected unless one of general deterioration. But my father lived to his eighty-third year with his mind as lively as ever it was, and all his faculties undimmed; and I hope that I may die before my mind fails to a sensible extent. I think that I have become a little more skilful in guessing right explanations and in devising experimental tests; but this may probably be the result of mere practice, and of a larger store of knowledge. I have as much difficulty as ever in expressing myself clearly and concisely; and this difficulty has caused me a very great loss of time; but it has had the compensating advantage of forcing me to think long and intently about

[103] Between November 1881 and February 1884, 8,500 copies were sold.—F. D.
[104] End of 1881 addendum. Beginning *"The Effects of Cross . . . ,"* p. 109.—N. B.

every sentence, and thus I have been often led to see errors in reasoning and in my own observations or those of others.

There seems to be a sort of fatality in my mind leading me to put at first my statement and proposition in a wrong or awkward form. Formerly I used to think about my sentences before writing them down; but for several years I have found that it saves time to scribble in a vile hand whole pages as quickly as I possibly can, contracting half the words; and then correct deliberately. Sentences thus scribbled down are often better ones than I could have written deliberately.

Having said this much about my manner of writing, I will add that with my larger books I spend a good deal of time over the general arrangement of the matter. I first make the rudest outline in two or three pages, and then a larger one in several pages, a few words or one word standing for a whole discussion or series of facts. Each of these headings is again enlarged and often transformed before I begin to write *in extenso*. As in several of my books facts observed by others have been very extensively used, and as I have always had several quite distinct subjects in hand at the same time, I may mention that I keep from thirty to forty large portfolios, in cabinets with labelled shelves, into which I can at once put a detached reference or memorandum. I have bought many books and at their ends I make an index of all the facts that concern my work; or, if the book is not my own, write out a separate abstract, and of such abstracts I have a large drawer full. Before beginning on any subject I look to all the short indexes and make a general and classified index, and by taking the one or more proper portfolios I have all the information collected during my life ready for use.

I have said that in one respect my mind has changed during the last twenty or thirty years. Up to the age of thirty, or beyond it, poetry of many kinds, such as the works of Milton, Gray, Byron, Wordsworth, Coleridge, and Shelley, gave me great pleasure, and even as a schoolboy I took intense delight in Shakespeare, especially in the historical plays. I have also said that formerly pictures gave me considerable, and music very great delight. But now for many years I cannot endure to read a line of poetry: I have tried lately to read Shakespeare, and found it so intolerably dull that it nauseated me. I have also almost lost any taste for pictures or music.—Music generally sets me thinking too energetically on what I have been at work on, instead of giving me pleasure. I retain some taste for fine scenery, but it does not cause me the exquisite delight which it formerly did. On the other hand, novels which are works of the imagination, though not of a very high order, have been for years a wonderful relief and pleasure to me, and I often bless all novelists. A surprising number have been read aloud to me, and I like all if moderately good, and if they do not end unhappily—against which a law ought to be passed. A novel, according to my taste, does not come into the first class unless it contains some person whom one can thoroughly love, and if it be a pretty woman all the better.

This curious and lamentable loss of the higher aesthetic tastes is all the odder, as books on history, biographies and travels (independently of any scientific facts which they may contain), and essays on all sorts of subjects interest me as much as ever they did. My mind seems to have become a kind of machine for grinding general laws out of large collections of facts, but why this should have caused the atrophy of that part of the brain alone, on which the higher tastes depend, I cannot conceive. A man with a mind more highly organised or better constituted than mine, would not I suppose have thus suffered; and if I had to live my life again I would have made a rule to read some poetry and listen to some music at least once every week; for perhaps the parts of my brain now atrophied could thus have been kept active through use. The loss of these tastes is a loss of happiness, and may possibly be injurious to the intellect, and more probably to the moral character, by enfeebling the emotional part of our nature.

My books have sold largely in England, have been translated

into many languages, and passed through several editions in foreign countries. I have heard it said that the success of a work abroad is the best test of its enduring value. I doubt whether this is at all trustworthy; but judged by this standard my name ought to last for a few years. Therefore it may be worth while for me to try to analyse the mental qualities and the conditions on which my success has depended; though I am aware that no man can do this correctly.

I have no great quickness of apprehension or wit which is so remarkable in some clever men, for instance Huxley. I am therefore a poor critic: a paper or book, when first read, generally excites my admiration, and it is only after considerable reflection that I perceive the weak points. My power to follow a long and purely abstract train of thought is very limited; I should, moreover, never have succeeded with metaphysics or mathematics. My memory is extensive, yet hazy: it suffices to make me cautious by vaguely telling me that I have observed or read something opposed to the conclusion which I am drawing, or on the other hand in favour of it; and after a time I can generally recollect where to search for my authority. So poor in one sense is my memory, that I have never been able to remember for more than a few days a single date or a line of poetry.

Some of my critics have said, "Oh, he is a good observer, but has no power of reasoning." I do not think that this can be true, for the *Origin of Species* is one long argument from the beginning to the end, and it has convinced not a few able men. No one could have written it without having some power of reasoning. I have a fair share of invention and of common sense or judgment, such as every fairly successful lawyer or doctor must have, but not I believe, in any higher degree.

On the favourable side of the balance, I think that I am superior to the common run of men in noticing things which easily escape attention, and in observing them carefully. My industry has been nearly as great as it could have been in the observation and collection of facts. What is far more important, my love of natural science has been steady and ardent. This pure love has, however, been much aided by the ambition to be esteemed by my fellow naturalists. From my early youth I have had the strongest desire to understand or explain whatever I observed,—that is, to group all facts under some general laws. These causes combined have given me the patience to reflect or ponder for any number of years over any unexplained problem. As far as I can judge, I am not apt to follow blindly the lead of other men. I have steadily endeavoured to keep my mind free, so as to give up any hypothesis, however much beloved (and I cannot resist forming one on every subject), as soon as facts are shown to be opposed to it. Indeed I have had no choice but to act in this manner, for with the exception of the Coral Reefs, I cannot remember a single first-formed hypothesis which had not after a time to be given up or greatly modified. This has naturally led me to distrust greatly deductive reasoning in the mixed sciences. On the other hand, I am not very sceptical,—a frame of mind which I believe to be injurious to the progress of science;[105] a good deal of scepticism in a scientific man is advisable to avoid much loss of time; for I have met with not a few men, who I feel sure have often thus been deterred from experiment or observations, which would have proved directly or indirectly serviceable.

In illustration, I will give the oddest case which I have known. A gentleman (who, as I afterwards heard, was a good local botanist) wrote to me from the Eastern counties that the seeds or beans of the common field-bean had this year every-where grown on the wrong side of the pod. I wrote back, asking for further information, as I did not understand what was meant; but I did not receive any answer for a long time. I then saw in two newspapers, one published in Kent and the other in

[105] Beginning of addendum. Addendum ends "which might be sold," p. 117. —N. B.

Yorkshire, paragraphs stating that it was a most remarkable fact that "the beans this year had all grown on the wrong side." So I thought that there must be some foundation for so general a statement. Accordingly, I went to my gardener, an old Kentish man, and asked him whether he had heard anything about it; and he answered, "Oh, no, Sir, it must be a mistake, for the beans grow on the wrong side only on Leap-year, and this is not Leap-year." I then asked him how they grew on common years and how on leap-years, but soon found out that he knew absolutely nothing of how they grew at any time; but he stuck to his belief.

After a time I heard from my first informant, who, with many apologies, said that he should not have written to me had he not heard the statement from several intelligent farmers; but that he had since spoken again to every one of them, and not one knew in the least what he had himself meant. So that here a belief—if indeed a statement with no definite idea attached to it can be called a belief—had spread over almost the whole of England without any vestige of evidence. I have known in the course of my life only three intentionally falsified statements, and one of these may have been a hoax (and there have been several scientific hoaxes) which, however, took in an American agricultural journal. It related to the formation in Holland of a new breed of oxen by the crossing of distinct species of Bos (some of which I happen to know are sterile together), and the author had the impudence to state that he had corresponded with me, and that I had been deeply impressed with the importance of his results. The article was sent to me by the editor of an English Agricult. Journal, asking for my opinion before republishing it.

A second case was an account of several varieties raised by the author from several species of Primula, which had spontaneously yielded a full complement of seed, although the parent plants had been carefully protected from the access of insects. This account was published before I had discovered the meaning of heterostylism, and the whole statement must have been fraudulent, or there was neglect in excluding insects so gross as to be scarcely credible.

The third case was more curious: Mr. Huth published in his book on Consanguineous Marriage some long extracts from a Belgian author, who stated that he had interbred rabbits in the closest manner for very many generations without the least injurious effects. The account was published in a most respectable Journal, that of the Royal Medical Soc. of Belgium; but I could not avoid feeling doubts,—I hardly know why, except that there were no accidents of any kind, and my experience in breeding animals made me think this improbable.

So with much hesitation I wrote to Prof. Van Beneden asking him whether the author was a trustworthy man. I soon heard in answer that the Society had been greatly shocked by discovering that the whole account was a fraud. The writer had been publicly challenged in the Journal to say where he had resided and kept his large stock of rabbits while carrying on his experiments, which must have consumed several years, and no answer could be extracted from him. I informed poor Mr. Huth, that the account which formed the cornerstone of his argument was fraudulent; and he in the most honourable manner immediately had a slip printed to this effect to be inserted in all future copies of his book which might be sold.[106]

My habits are methodical, and this has been of not a little use for my particular line of work. Lastly, I have had ample leisure from not having to earn my own bread. Even ill-health, though it has annihilated several years of my life, has saved me from the distractions of society and amusement.

Therefore, my success as a man of science, whatever this may have amounted to, has been determined, as far as I can judge, by complex and diversified mental qualities and conditions. Of

[106] End of undated addendum of 5 1/2 paragraphs.—N. B.

these the most important have been—the love of science—
unbounded patience in long reflecting over any subject—industry in observing and collecting facts—and a fair share of
invention as well as of common-sense. With such moderate abilities as I possess, it is truly surprising that thus I should have
influenced to a considerable extent the beliefs of scientific men
on some important points.

August 3rd 1876

*This sketch of my life was begun about May 28th. at Hopedene, and since
then I have written for nearly an hour on most afternoons*

APPENDIX

PART ONE

On Charles Darwin and his Grandfather Dr. Erasmus Darwin

THE INHERENT similarities between Charles and Erasmus Darwin, born seventy-eight years apart, with a period of convulsive social and intellectual history between them, makes some comparison of the fate of their respective achievements in the world of thought of particular interest. For Erasmus Darwin, like his grandson, formulated an evolutionary system of world order, yet left no lasting mark on commonly held beliefs. Charles succeeded where Erasmus had failed; and in this Appendix I have attempted to show some of the reasons why.

Dr. Erasmus Darwin (1731–1802) lived under a dwindling Church authority, with science and philosophy announcing the approaching perfectibility of Man. It was a period of belief in material progress, when the steam engine, the mechanisation of industry, canals and sewage works, seemed symbols of Man's power over external nature. The newly discovered laws of physics and the emerging laws in the world of chemistry, gave a further sense of confidence. Natural Theology was being preached by Paley and others, who not only took into account the increasing knowledge of adaptation in biology, but made a pivot of this very knowledge. Dr. Darwin looked at the facts of adaptation in the human body without the bias so general in 18th century science,—a bias which saw a purpose in all the Creator's works for the immediate benefit of mankind; he produced his original theory of Generation or Descent with modification in his *Zoönomia* in

1794–6, partially anticipating Lamarck's better-known theory, and preceding him by fifteen years.

Today it is difficult to realise the immense vogue Erasmus Darwin's works once possessed, but when Charles was young the imposing memory of his grandfather must still have loomed large. Today *Zoönomia* is tough reading, whilst the heroic couplets of *The Botanic Garden and Phytologia*, with their repeated evocations of Deities and Nymphs, are easy subjects for parody; the voluminous prose notes which contain the overflow of his copious ideas make better reading. Years before Charles was born, Coleridge coined the word "darwinising" to describe the wild theorising of Erasmus,—though some of these ideas had affected Coleridge deeply in his youth, when still in sympathy with scientific adventure. It was only in his later years of disillusionment and antagonism to contemporary materialism that he came to oppose all that Erasmus Darwin stood for and cried:—"O Mercy, the blindness of the man!" Erasmus's poetry nauseated him, and he likened his verse to "the mists that occasionally arise at the foot of Parnassus"; and he stigmatised Dr. Darwin's philosophy in *Zoönomia* as the "State of Nature or the Orang Outang theology of the human race, substituted for the first chapters of the Book of Genesis";—a strange foreshadowing of the outraged protests that followed on the publication of the *Origin of Species* two generations later.

Many of the other subjects besides the theory of Descent dealt with in *Zoönomia*, became favourite themes for Charles's intensive study later on. Of course the topics discussed by them both have an older history, and Linnaeus, Buffon and others helped to fix attention on certain matters, such as the changes occurring in domesticated animals. In *Zoönomia* Erasmus considers the twining and other movements in plants; the cross-fertilisation in plants; the origin of the sense of beauty in connection with the female form; adaptive and protective coloration, heredity, and the domestication of animals. Charles Darwin deals with these subjects in the following books;—*Climbing Plants*; *Power of Movement of Plants*; *Cross- and Self-Fertilisation in Plants*; *Fertilisation of Orchids*; *Descent of Man*; *Variation of Animals and Plants under Domestication*; and the *Origin of Species*.

Erasmus Darwin wrote of sexual selection:—"The final cause of this contest among males seems to be, that the strongest and most active animal should propagate the species which should thus become improved." This might be mistaken for a sentence written by Charles himself sixty-five years later; for here Erasmus has groped towards the idea of selection.

Yet it will have been noted in *The Autobiography* (p. 43) that Charles insists that neither Lamarck's writings nor his grandfather's had had any effect on him. The apparent contradiction implicit in his admission following this assertion, that hearing such views maintained early in life may have favoured his upholding them "in a different form" may, I believe, be understood by emphasising the words "*in a different form.*" For Erasmus Darwin's method was largely built of a heavy superstructure of speculation on an insufficient foundation of fact, a method alien to Charles Darwin's whole outlook. Charles was asking new questions of life's processes and saw a general pattern emerging through the agency of Natural Selection; Nature and her myriad forms became a possible self-regulating system,—though the central mystery of the living reproducing unit remained. The conviction of the power of Natural Selection, working on the universality of variation in animals and plants, led Charles to reject early evolutionary influences as the mere facile speculations of a *priori* philosophers, who saw a Creation for Man's use in all Nature's Works. What Charles was advocating in his own work was theory built on a firmer structure of evidence. He vindicated a new balance in Natural Science between theory and a more scrupulous observation of fact, and a more rigorous recourse to experiment. The strength of his argument in the *Origin of Species*,—and indeed in all his work—lay in his power of generalisation under the strictest control of related observations; a generalisation became "a short-hand expression with predictive power."[107]

In a letter to Charles Lyell written in 1859, he wrote of Lamarck's work that he got "not a fact or idea from it." Such a disclaimer can only mean that to Charles Darwin the absence of evidence for Lamarck's theory invalidated the whole, in the same way that his grandfather's theory was invalidated. But although Charles remained suspicious of his grandfather's "overpowering tendency to theorise and generalise," he nevertheless added this tribute to Erasmus in his *Life of Erasmus Darwin*; "His remarks . . . on the value of experiments and the use of hypotheses show that he had the true spirit of the philosopher."

Charles denied too that the subject of evolution was in the air, (*Autobiography,* p. 101) but again it was the facts, "the innumerable well-observed facts" which were lacking. No doubt the isolation of life at Down must have helped to prevent the penetration of opinion from workers in other fields than his own, so that he unconsciously overlooked indications that belief in the permanence of species was waning. In this context it is worth quoting the young Bostonian intellectual Henry Brooks Adams, who knew England well in the 1860's—especially diplomatic England—when he was acting as private secretary to his father, the American Minister. Young Adams was born in 1838, under the shadow of Bostonian Unitarianism, and in the chapter of his autobiography entitled *Darwinism,*[108] Adams reveals contemporary opinion, and says "he felt, like nine men in ten an instinctive belief in Evolution." He writes:—"At that moment ('67) Darwin was convulsing society.

The geological champion of Darwin was Sir Charles Lyell, and the Lyells were intimate at the Legation. Sir Charles constantly

---

[107] J. O. Wisdom. Foundation of Inference in Natural Science.
[108] *The Education of Henry Adams. An Autobiography.* 1918. Henry Adams always speaks of himself in the third person.

said of Darwin, what Palgrave said of Tennyson, that the first time he came to town, Adams should be asked to meet him, but neither of them ever came to town, or ever cared to meet a young American, and one could not go to them because they were known to dislike intrusion. The only Americans who were not allowed to intrude were the half-dozen in the Legation. Adams was content to read Darwin, specially his *Origin of Species* and his *Voyage of the Beagle*. He was a Darwinist before the letter; a predestined follower of the tide; but he was hardly trained to follow Darwin's evidences. . . . He never tried to understand Darwin; but he still fancied he might get the best part of Darwinism from the easier study of geology; a science which suited idle minds as well as though it were history. Every curate in England dabbled in geology and hunted only for vestiges of Creation. Darwin hunted for vestiges of Natural Selection, and Adams followed him, although he cared nothing about Selection, unless for the indirect amusement of upsetting curates. He felt, like nine men in ten, an instinctive belief in Evolution, but he felt no more concern in Natural than in unnatural Selection . . ."

This was written after Darwin had "convulsed society"; but there are earlier significant examples, showing how well-founded ideas had long been in the air, though Charles Darwin may not have known of them.

In the sphere of social history before Malthus gained publicity for his views, there were others who saw how the struggle for existence was actually affecting populations. Halévy, in his *History of the English People*, refers to an obscure pamphlet on the Poor Laws, by a "Well-wisher to Mankind," written in 1786. The writer, the Rev. Mr. Townsend, blames the Poor Laws for preserving the weak at the expense of the strong, with all the implications of the working of Natural Selection. He takes the analogy of the populations of goats and greyhounds on the island of Juan Fernandez, mentioned by Dampier. The goats at first were in sole possession and reached a subsistence level in the face of some disease and the raids

of English Privateers. Then the Spaniards put a pair of greyhounds on the island to extirpate the goats and annoy the English. These greyhounds "increased in proportion to the quantity of
food they met with." The goats diminished and retired to the
rocks, and a new balance was set up; "the weakest of both species
were amongst the first to pay the debt of nature, the most active
and vigorous preserved their lives. It is the quantity of food which
regulates the number of the human species . . . the weak must
depend on the precarious bounty of the strong . . ."

But Darwin did admit in the passage from the *Autobiography*
(p. 102), that "innumerable well-observed facts were stored in the
minds of naturalists ready to take their proper place as soon as any
theory which would receive them was sufficiently explained."
These words exactly fit the case of a younger contemporary of
Darwin's, to whom the joint paper by Wallace and Darwin in the
Linnean Journal in 1858 came as a revelation of light, so that the
stored well-observed facts fell into place.

Alfred Newton, Professor of comparative anatomy at Cambridge from 1866–1907, was one of the first naturalists to accept
the evolutionary theory on its new basis of Natural Selection, as a
welcome solution to the many problems of bird distribution, variation and adaptation, which had long been puzzling him.[109]

In 1858 he had been with John Wolley in Iceland, and enforced
idleness had led to frequent discussions on the old topics of species,
their origins and limits. Years later, in February 1888, he published an article in Macmillan's Magazine entitled *The Early Days
of Darwinism*, in which he describes the immediate and over-
whelming effect on his mind produced by reading the joint paper
by Wallace and Darwin. He writes:—"Not many days after my
return home (from Iceland) there reached me the part of the Journal of the Linnean Society which bears on its cover the date 20th

[109] See *Life of Alfred Newton*, by A. F. R. Wollaston, John Murray, 1921.

August, 1858, and contains the papers of Mr. Darwin and Mr. Wallace. . . . I sat up late that night to read it; and never shall I forget the impression it made upon me. Herein was contained a perfectly simple solution of all the difficulties which had been troubling me for months past. I hardly knew whether I at first felt more vexed at the solution not having occurred to me than pleased that it had been found at all. However, after reading these papers more than once, I went to bed satisfied that a solution had been found. All personal feeling apart, it came to me like the direct revelation of a higher power; and I awoke next morning with the consciousness that there was an end of all the mystery in the simple phrase "Natural Selection." I am free to confess that in my joy I did not then perceive, and I cannot say when I did begin to perceive, that though my especial puzzles were thus explained, dozens, scores, nay hundreds of other difficulties lay in the path."

To Charles Darwin it was the body of evidence supporting evolutionary theory that mattered, and that he knew was his own contribution. Neither his grandfather, nor any of his contemporaries, saving only A. R. Wallace, had looked both closely enough at the smallest detail, and broadly enough at the vast procession of organic form, to bring this authoritative evidence to bear, without which he could admit no influence to his mind.

The love of close observation of natural fact and his need for a theory to explain everything he saw, forms the closely woven tissue which constituted his genius. It is worth considering a certain change of emphasis in the warp and the weft of his scientific thinking that takes place as the years pass. As a young man his suspicion of the speculative philosopher was unqualified; in later years he acknowledged a growing respect for speculation, if well followed up by observation and experiment. Sometimes he uses the words *generalisation* and *speculation* loosely, but *generalisation* towards the end of his life reaches respectability if backed by a sufficient body of factual evidence. This change followed the course of his intellectual development; his theorising instinct, never absent,[1] was at first held on a tight rein, which was only slackened as his power of drawing inferences increased with the increase of his knowledge. Fact-seeking and theory often seem almost welded as one process in his mind; yet sometimes he discriminates clearly. Though the theory is worthless without the well-observed facts, the facts are useless without the frame of the theory to receive them. He agreed with Buffon's well-known advice to study the How of things, and not the Why; but he did not agree with another recommendation—"Ramassons des faits pour nous donner des idées." For Darwin came to believe that the value of fact-finding lies solely in relation to theory. This may seem a contradiction to his mistrust of speculation as a danger to scientific thought which I have insisted on; I believe that his development from the youthful pleasure in direct observation and collecting to the maturer satisfaction of the theorist, can largely account for the inconsistency.

I am giving quotations from his letters at different periods of his life to establish this alteration of stress. A certain vacillation is also shown; it could not well be otherwise, since all scientific work requires both theory and fact-finding. Moreover his different correspondents needed varying advice. Nevertheless I think there is a general trend in his thought from the early fear of wild speculation towards a mature appreciation of theory on a factual basis. This relates the quotations to the argument of this Appendix; Darwin's denial both of his grandfather's influence and of the importance of earlier evolutionists was really a repudiation of their premises and method of attack.

QUOTATIONS

Emma Darwin used to repeat this saying of her husband's:—"It is a fatal fault to reason whilst observing, though so necessary beforehand and so useful afterwards." This piece of advice is worth recording as in some measure summing up Charles's views given in the following quotations.

In 1837, soon after his return from the *Beagle* voyage, he wrote amongst stray jotted notes, given in full in Note 3, p. 194:—"I have so much more pleasure in direct observation that I could not go on as Lyell does, correcting and adding up new information to old train and I do not see what line can be followed by man tied down to London.—In country—experiment and observation on lower animals." In another place on the same page he writes:— "Systematize and study affinities." Thus in 1837 he recognized the stimulus that was to persist to the end of his life from his delight in direct observation. But the two words "study affinities" show that a background of theory was there, and that his mind was already in travail with evolutionary problems.

In 1844 he wrote to J. D. Hooker, (*More Letters*, Vol. I, p. 39.) "I must be allowed to put my own interpretation on what you say of 'not being a good arranger of extended views'—which is that you do not indulge in the loose speculations so easily started by every smatterer and wandering collector. I look at a strong tendency to generalise as an entire evil."

In 1850 he wrote to C. H. L. Woodd on heat effects in geological stratification. (*More Letters*, Vol. II, p. 133.) "All young geologists have a great turn for speculation; I have burnt my fingers pretty sharply in that way, and am now perhaps becoming over-cautious; and feel inclined to cavil at speculation when the direct and immediate effect of a cause in question cannot be shewn. . . . I can have no doubt that speculative men, with a curb on, make far the best observers . . . With every good wish that you may go on with your geological studies, speculations, and especially observations."

In 1857 he wrote to Asa Gray, (*More Letters*, Vol. II, p. 252.), who he thought was not indulging enough in generalisation. He began to emphasise the hardness of observation, by which I think is implied the difficulty for the theoriser to keep the integrity of impartiality; the facts are of value in relation to the theory, and therefore prejudice is easy.

"Now I would say it is your duty to generalise as far as you safely can from your as yet completed work. . . . As careful observation is far harder work than generalisation, and still harder than speculation, do you not think it very possible that it may be overvalued? It ought never to be forgotten that the observer can generalise his own observations incomparably better than anyone else. How many astronomers have laboured their whole lives on observations, and have not drawn a single conclusion; I think it is Herschel who has remarked how much better it would be if they had paused in their devoted work and seen what they could have deduced from their work."

In 1861 in his letter to Henry Fawcett (More Letters, Vol. I, p. 195) he acknowledges that observation is itself a selective act. "How odd it is that anyone should not see that all observation must be for or against some view if it is to be of any service!" Here he admits that there must be a "view" preceding observation, that is, a theory or hypothesis which lends value to the fact-finding.[110]

In 1863 he wrote to J. Scott (More Letters, Vol. II, p. 323): "I would suggest to you the advantage, at present, of being very sparing in introducing theory in your papers (I formerly erred much in Geology in that way): *let theory guide your observations*, but till your reputation is well established, be sparing in publishing theory. It makes persons doubt your observations."

In 1870 he wrote to J. D. Hooker (More Letters, Vol. I, p. 321.) "Your conclusion that all speculation about preordination is idle waste of time is the only wise one; but how difficult it is not to speculate! My theology is a simple muddle; I cannot look at the universe as the result of blind chance, yet I can see no evidence of beneficent design, or indeed of design of any kind, in the details."

[110] Quoted by J. O. Wisdom, *Foundations of Inference in Natural Science*.

He summarised his view of deductive writing in his comment on Herbert Spencer. "His deductive manner of treating every subject is wholly opposed to my frame of mind . . . over and over again have I said to myself after reading one of his discussions— 'Here would be a fine subject for half a dozen years' work.' "

His son Francis wrote in *Life and Letters* (Vol. I, p. 149), on his father's attitude to theory and observation towards the end of his life. After dwelling on his father's repeatedly saying that it was important to know when to give up an enquiry, Francis Darwin continues:—"He often said that no one could be a good observer unless he was an active theoriser. This brings me back to what I said about his instinct for arresting exceptions: it was as though he were charged with theorising power ready to flow into any channel on the slightest disturbance, so that no fact, however small, could avoid releasing a stream of theory, and thus the fact became magnified into importance. In this way it naturally happened that many untenable theories occurred to him; but fortunately his richness of imagination was equalled by his power of judging and condemning the thoughts that occurred to him."

Here Francis describes the essential richness of ideas and speculative power in his father, without which the fact-finding censor of the mind has nothing to work on; only then can the censor afford to discard untenable hypotheses or ideas for a new speculative pattern. The "right" one is the one to fit the greatest number of facts.

The last quotation in the chronological list of letters shows how Charles was still speculating on this intricate interlocking of the two processes towards the end of his life. I give the whole characteristic letter in which the passage occurs written to his youngest son Horace on the occasion of his passing the Little Go at Cambridge at the age of 20 in 1871. Horace had not been brilliant at school or university, and examinations were dreaded.

6 Q. Anne St.

Friday morning 8.30 *a.m.*   W.

[*Dec.* 15 1871]

My Dear Horace,

We are so rejoiced, for we have just had a card from that good George in Cambridge, saying that you are all right and safe through the accursed Little Go.—I am so glad, and now you can follow the bent of your talents and work as hard at Mathematicks and science, as your health will permit.

I have been speculating last night what makes a man a discoverer of undiscovered things, and a most perplexing problem it is.—Many men who are very clever,—much cleverer than discoverers—never originate anything. As far as I can conjecture, the art consists in habitually searching for causes or meaning of everything which occurs. This implies sharp observation and requires as much knowledge as possible of the subject investigated.

But why I write all this now, I hardly know,—except out of the fullness of my heart; for I do rejoice heartily that you have passed this Charybdis.—

Your affectionate Father

C. Darwin

I have stressed the importance of Charles's changing views on speculation in his intellectual development, for it seems to me clear that he made use of his opposition to his father's and grandfather's mode of thought to vindicate his own independence. Robert's severe criticism of Charles as a young man could thus be claimed as an integral step in the story of his son's development; without the urgent need to claim independence, would Charles have wished to overcome Robert's opposition to the proposed *Beagle* voyage? Without that five-years' discipline, would Charles's genius have come to fruition? Conjectures can be endless; but to me no reference to Robert's tyranny, nor to the early death of

Charles's mother, can solve the particular problems of this Appendix.[111] The impact of contemporary ideas and opinions handed on from the mature to the younger generation, will always be accompanied by unpredictable emotional reactions, often unrecognised, and perhaps all the more intense where there is no violent schism in a family tradition for an open break-away.

Charles's devotion to his father Robert might have kept him in bondage longer than was the case. Though there was no publication on evolution until after his father's death, Charles was nevertheless working his way to freedom years earlier. A vindication of intellectual independence from his grandfather's scientific method and his father's dominating personality lay along the same path,—namely the scientific path of a search for factual evidence. Dr. Robert, though without the scientific mind, was given to speculation on every subject, like his own father Erasmus; so that in repudiating the way of thought of one ancestor, Charles was really rejecting both. It has been suggested that he dropped the profession of medicine as part of this rejection of the ancestral attitudes. Medicine may well have seemed to Charles too closely associated with a "speculative" turn of mind.

In conclusion I should like to stress again the similarity and dissimilarity between Charles and Erasmus Darwin; their interests and family traditions ran parallel, yet there was a wide divergence in their basic characters and in their reactions to the contemporary scene. Charles Darwin had been brought up on the traditions and opinions of the early 19th century when the rationalism and utilitarian outlook of the 18th century still reigned. Dr. Erasmus Darwin had been a mouthpiece for that earlier period of enthusiasm when unknown animals and plants were reaching Europe through increased trade and travel, and Linnaeus was leading biologic nomenclature out of chaos. Throughout Europe a closer scrutiny

[111] See Note 5 on Charles's ill-health, p. 201. The extent of Robert's tyranny may be questioned.

of living forms was put in motion; old scientific sign-posts were done away with, and Erasmus was one of the pioneers who installed a new one pointing to Evolution. Two generations later it was his grandson Charles's turn to express new ideas, built on new knowledge. It became his turn to correct old sign-posts, and his grandfather's was one of those he repainted. On the newer sign-post was again the word Evolution, but he added Natural Selection as a pointer how to get there. More significant than a direction to any final goal, was the clear guidance on how to read the map.

PART TWO

The Darwin-Butler Controversy

TODAY THE ONCE notorious quarrel between Samuel Butler and Charles Darwin is almost forgotten, and the short account in the complete version of the *Autobiography*,—printed here for the first time,—will only raise vague memories in the minds of most readers.

The story is a complex one, both in substance and chronology, but after I had examined the wealth of material among the Darwin MSS. in the Cambridge University Library the whole incident appeared to me in such a new light that I felt it must be retold in all its detail. In the old letters from this full dossier voices from the past speak out, upholding Darwin's case against Butler and advising silence; whatever may be thought now of this advice, the voices of Charles's devoted friends and relations all declared Samuel Butler's attacks to be unjustified and base.

Samuel Butler was twenty-six years younger than Charles Darwin, and as a young sheep-farmer in New Zealand he watched the battle waged against orthodoxy soon after the publication of the *Origin of Species* with the enthusiasm of a proselyte. The letters to Darwin of this period, humble, sincere and filled with admiration, are also in the Cambridge dossier, and form a revealing contrast to his later bitter indictments. The mutual attraction and friendly correspondence soon began to cool; as Darwin's star rose for the scientific world, so did it sink in Butler's estimation. For Butler never really understood the full importance of Darwin's revolution in scientific thinking. Believing that Mind is the controller of evolutionary direction, he began to study the early evolutionists, Buffon, Dr. Erasmus Darwin and Lamarck, and the more he studied them, the more he liked them and disliked the younger upstart Darwin. Butler, in attempting to reinstate the older evolutionists, aligned himself with the 18th century, so that the quarrel becomes intimately bound up with Charles's judgment of his grandfather's views which I have already discussed; the controversy between them is in fact another aspect of the change taking place in biological thinking towards the middle of the 19th century.

The chronology of certain publications in 1879 is of importance in understanding the climax of Butler's increasing antagonism.

On Charles Darwin's seventieth birthday in February 1879, there was issued in Germany a congratulatory number of the German periodical *Kosmos* (II, Jahrg. Heft II), containing an article by Dr. E. Krause on Dr. Erasmus Darwin's contribution towards the history of the Descent-theory. In May, 1879, Butler published *Evolution Old and New, or the Theories of Buffon, Dr. Erasmus Darwin and Lamarck compared with that of Mr. C. Darwin*, without being aware of Krause's article in *Kosmos*. Meanwhile Krause was enlarging his essay for translation; it formed the second part of Charles Darwin's *Life of Erasmus Darwin*, published in November of the same year. Whilst Krause had been engaged in this collaboration, Charles had sent him a copy of Butler's work, and some of Krause's additions consisted of disparaging references to Butler's ideas. The main offending passage ran:—"Erasmus Darwin's system was in itself a most significant first step in the path which his grandson has opened up for us, but to wish to revive it at the present day as has actually been attempted, shows a weakness of thought and a mental anachronism which no one can envy."

Unfortunately Charles Darwin's Preface to his *Life of Erasmus Darwin* omitted to state that Krause's original essay had been

altered—exactly how this happened is explained later.[112] Butler
soon compared the supposed correct translation with a copy of the
original, and the differences led him to conclude that the unac-
knowledged alterations formed a covert attack against himself;
the public would think his views had been condemned, even
before the publication of *Evolution Old and New*, and by an independent German scholar.

Charles apologised to Butler on realizing his error of omission,
but Butler's conviction that he was the victim of a plot stood firm.
His intense emotional virulence—together with the advice of
Darwin's relations and friends—finally suffocated Darwin into
silence, in spite of his original determination to give a succinct
account of how his mistake had arisen.

What was really at stake in this storm in a tea-cup? The Victorian security, which seems so solid as we look back, is here seen
rocking. Darwin and Butler both craved for approbation; Darwin,
in his anxiety and distress at Butler's attacks, needed the approval
of family and intimate friends to allow him to withdraw from the
pain of controversy into his evolutionary stronghold,—won with
no failure of courage in the face of opposition some twenty years
earlier. He was sure of himself where scientific questions were at
stake, but needed protection against human antagonisms. Butler
had faced opposition all his life, and courted it as the aggressive
do; but he too needed approval and his faithful friend, Miss Savage, was always ready to sanction his revenge by playing on the
theme of the villainy of the Darwin clique and their monstrous
humbug. The intensity of Butler's feeling is expressed in his first
letter to the *Athenæum* which will be given in full later, in which
he says: "It is doubtless a common practice for writers to take an
opportunity of revising their works, but it is not common when a
covert condemnation of an opponent has been interpolated into a
revised edition, the revision of which has been concealed, to

[112] See p. 149, Festing Jones's Pamphlet, Proposed letter No. I.

declare with every circumstance of distinctness that the condemnation was written prior to the book which might appear to have called it forth, and thus lead readers to suppose that it must be an unbiased opinion."

Readers of the 1887 version of the *Autobiography* will find no reference to the quarrel in any words of Charles's. It is significant that Francis Darwin omitted all mention by his father of the quarrel when he was editing the *Autobiography* in *Life and Letters* in 1887, for it was Francis who had urged that a public explanation should be made at the time of Butler's bitterest attacks. Perhaps the family censorship that had exercised discretion over the religious passages was again at work; perhaps family feelings were still too raw in 1887 for the question to be opened up afresh. Francis makes a reference to the incident in Vol. III of *Life and Letters*, p. 220, where he says: "The publication of the '*Life of Erasmus Darwin*' led to an attack by Mr. Samuel Butler, which amounted to a charge of falsehood against my father. After consulting his friends, he came to the determination to leave the charge unanswered as being unworthy of his notice. . . . The affair gave my father much pain, but the warm sympathy of those whose opinion he respected soon helped him to let it pass into a well-merited oblivion."

The letters in the Cambridge University Library are concerned with the notice Darwin should or should not take of Samuel Butler's assaults, including the judgments of T. H. Huxley and Leslie Stephen, which have not been published before. Darwin wrote at the very outset: "I have resolved to send one [a reply] as I can say something in defence of my negligence." It is the story of how he yielded to his advisers that I give fully, the ensuing silence only serving to confirm Butler in his persecution mania, so that his anger exploded in a vacuum. Charles Darwin was prevailed on not to answer the attacks against his own first instinct for reasons that turned mainly on saving his dignity. This Butler perceived; and anything that seemed to him shrouded in reverence was worth a shot. However basely he construed the silence, the fact remains that he never got a clear and complete account of how the mistake and the muddle in the Preface of the *Life of Erasmus Darwin* had originated.

Henry Festing Jones, Butler's biographer and friend, brought out a Pamphlet in 1911, now out of print, entitled *Charles Darwin and Samuel Butler, A Step toward Reconciliation*. Francis Darwin had helped to bring about this reconciliation by telling what he knew, and producing documents that Festing Jones had not seen. Neither had Francis Darwin seen Butler's Preface to the 2nd edition of *Evolution Old and New*, written in April 1882, on hearing of the death of Charles Darwin. In it Butler's enmity and sense of injury are subdued in the common sorrow; Festing Jones read it to Francis Darwin when they met in 1910 to discuss the Pamphlet. Had this Preface, with its reasonable tone, come to Francis Darwin's notice, the last twenty years of Butler's feud with Darwin must have run another course. But Butler died in 1902, with this tragic misunderstanding still unresolved. Francis Darwin always regretted that he had not gone to him and had their differences out face to face in the early days of the quarrel.

I felt it necessary to incorporate the Pamphlet, though this involves me in a certain repetition of the narrative. But the case in defence of Butler, written by his biographer and friend, cannot be omitted by anyone deeply interested in this network of personal Victorian history. The new material from Cambridge revealed more than appeared in the Pamphlet alone, and I have therefore made the whole story accessible by adding the new unpublished letters at the end of the Pamphlet *en bloc*, marking their chronological position by footnotes.

The exchange of letters to and from Down, some of which were sent to London by road in the Down carriage, with John the coachman waiting to bring back the answers, shows how serious was the flutter in the Darwin Dove-cot. The family rhyme:—

"Write a letter, write a letter,
Good advice will make us better,"

could not have been more explicitly obeyed.

In the following reprint of the Pamphlet (pp. 141–164), my
additions such as supplementary footnotes, are in square brackets.
The new unpublished letters A to L follow, pp. 168–182; and in
conclusion, a brief summary is given.

CHARLES DARWIN AND SAMUEL BUTLER
A STEP TOWARDS RECONCILIATION

Published by A. C. Fifield, 1911

Those who have read Samuel Butler's books, *Life and Habit*, *Evolution Old and New*, *Unconscious Memory*, and *Luck or Cunning?* are aware that he did not agree entirely with Charles Darwin on the subject of evolution. They also know that there was a personal quarrel between the two men of which the story is told in Chapter IV of *Unconscious Memory*. This story has appeared to some of Butler's readers to be so strange, and to some of Darwin's admirers so improbable, especially in regard to the conclusions which Butler drew, that they have felt there must be an explanation. A correspondence has recently taken place between Mr. Francis Darwin and myself, and he has sent to me, as Butler's biographer, some letters which throw light upon the controversy. From these, and from what has passed between us, I have taken information for the Memoir of Butler which I am writing, but as this Memoir may not be finished for some time, and not published for some time longer, and Mr. Francis Darwin agrees with me that in justice both to Charles Darwin and to Butler, the explanation of what really occurred should be made public as soon as possible, I have written the following pages for immediate publication. Mr. F. Darwin has read the MS., and had kindly made various suggestions of which I have taken advantage. He differs entirely from nearly all Butler's opinions as here given (I did not expect him to agree with them); nevertheless, he is good enough to express himself as grateful for the manner in which I have accepted and utilised the material supplied by him. And I am grateful to him for having made it possible for me to clear up an unfortunate misunderstanding.

The friendship between the families of Darwin and Butler began many years ago. Charles Darwin's father, Robert, was the leading doctor in Shrewsbury when Butler's grandfather, Dr. Butler, was headmaster of Shrewsbury School. Charles Darwin and Butler's father, Canon Butler, were schoolfellows at Shrewsbury, under Dr. Butler, and undergraduates together at Cambridge. They spent the summer of 1828 together on a reading-party at Barmouth, and Canon Butler said of Charles Darwin, "He inoculated me with a taste for Botany which has stuck by me all my life." (*Life and Letters of Charles Darwin*, by his son, Francis Darwin, Vol. I, 168).

The *Origin of Species* appeared in 1859 and Butler read the book in New Zealand. "I became one of Mr. Darwin's many enthusiastic admirers, and wrote a philosophic dialogue (the most offensive form, except poetry and books of travel into supposed unknown countries, that even literature can assume) upon the *Origin of Species*. This production appeared in *The Press*, Canterbury, in 1861 or 1862, but I have long lost the only copy I ever had" (*Unconscious Memory*, Chapter I, p. 17).[113] In 1872, when Butler published *Erewhon*, which is his own book of travel into a supposed unknown country, he wrote to Charles Darwin to explain what he meant by "The Book of the Machines": "I am sincerely sorry that some of the critics should have thought I was laughing at your theory, a thing which I never meant to do, and should be shocked at having done."

Soon after this he paid two visits to Mr. Darwin at Down, and thus became acquainted with all the family. Mr. Francis Darwin

[113 Reprinted in R. A. Streatfeild's *A First Year in Canterbury Settlement*, 1923, p. 155.]

and Butler saw a great deal of one another from this time until 1877–8, when Butler published *Life and Habit*. While he was writing this book Mr. Francis Darwin called upon him, and spoke of Hering's theory, which refers all life to memory. "He came September 26th, 1877" (*Unconscious Memory*, Chapter II). In *Life and Habit* (December, 1877) it began to appear that Butler was dissatisfied with much in Charles Darwin's writings, but there was as yet no open breach between him and the Darwins.

In February, 1879, a German scientific journal called *Kosmos* published an article by Dr. Krause about the Life and Works of Dr. Erasmus Darwin.

In May, 1879, Butler, who had not then heard of the article, published *Evolution, Old and New, or The Theories of Buffon, Dr. Erasmus Darwin and Lamarck as compared with that of Mr. Charles Darwin*. One of the objects of this book was to show that the idea of descent with modification did not originate with Charles Darwin; and another was to restore mind to the universe, for Butler thought that the tendency of Charles Darwin's writings was to give too much prominence to accident at the expense of design in his theory of evolution.

Mr. Darwin sent a copy of Butler's book to Dr. Krause, because it was about Erasmus Darwin, and he knew that Dr. Krause was revising his article for translation into English, but he hoped he would "not expend much powder and shot on Mr. Butler, for he really is not worthy of it. His work is merely ephemeral."

Dr. Krause went on revising his article, and in November, 1879, Mr. Murray published *Erasmus Darwin, by Ernst Krause, translated from the German by W. S. Dallas, with a preliminary notice by Charles Darwin*. It appears from the preface that Dr. Krause's part of this book consists of his sketch of Erasmus Darwin, which had appeared in *Kosmos*, and of which he had allowed Charles Darwin and his brother Erasmus to have a translation made. On this there is a footnote as follows:—

Mr. Dallas has undertaken the translation, and his scientific reputation, together with his knowledge of German, is a guarantee for its accuracy.

The preface goes on to say that Charles Darwin, having private materials for adding to the knowledge of Erasmus Darwin's character, had written a preliminary notice. Particulars are given, two books (Miss Seward's *Life of Dr. Darwin* and Dr. Dowson's *Lecture on Erasmus Darwin*) are mentioned, and at the end of the preface is this second footnote:—

Since the publication of Dr. Krause's article Mr. Butler's work *Evolution Old and New*, 1879, has appeared, and this includes an account of Dr. Darwin's life, compiled from the two books just mentioned, and of his views on evolution.

Butler read *Erasmus Darwin* in English and, knowing nothing of the revision, was puzzled. He sent to Germany for the *Kosmos* of February, 1879, and was more puzzled. He wrote to Mr. Darwin on the 2nd January, 1880, asking for an explanation—"an explanation which," as he says in Chapter IV of *Unconscious Memory*, "I would have gladly strained a good many points to have accepted"—and Mr. Darwin replied the next day. These are the two letters:—

Samuel Butler to Charles Darwin

January 2nd, 1880

Dear Sir,

Will you kindly refer me to the edition of *Kosmos* which contains the text of Dr. Krause's article on Dr. Erasmus Darwin, as translated by Mr. W. S. Dallas?

I have before me the last February number of *Kosmos*, which appears by your preface to be the one from which Mr. Dallas has translated, but his translation contains long and important passages which are not in the February number of *Kosmos*, while many passages in the original are omitted in the translation.

Among the passages introduced are the last six pages of the English article, which seem to condemn by anticipation the position I have taken as regards Erasmus Darwin in my book *Evolution Old and New*, and which I believe I was the first to take. The concluding, and therefore, perhaps, most prominent sentence of the translation you have given to the public stands thus:—

"Erasmus Darwin's system was in itself a most significant first step in the path of knowledge his grandson has opened up for us, but to wish to revive it at the present day, as has actually been seriously attempted, shows a weakness of thought and a mental anachronism which no one can envy."

The *Kosmos* which has been sent me from Germany contains no such passage.

As you have stated in your preface that my book, *Evolution Old and New*, appeared subsequently to Dr. Krause's article, and as no intimation is given that the article has been altered and added to since its original appearance, while the accuracy of the translation, as though from the February number of *Kosmos* is, as you expressly say, guaranteed by Mr. Dallas's "scientific reputation, together with his knowledge of German," your readers will naturally suppose that all they read in the translation appeared in February last, and therefore before *Evolution Old and New* was written, and therefore independently of, and necessarily without reference to, that book.

I do not doubt that this was actually the case, but have failed to obtain the edition which contains the passage above referred to, and several others which appear in the translation.

I have a personal interest in this matter, and venture, therefore, to ask for the explanation, which I do not doubt you will readily give me.—Yours faithfully, S. BUTLER

Charles Darwin to Samuel Butler

January 3rd, 1880

My dear Sir,

Dr. Krause, soon after the appearance of his article in *Kosmos*, told me that he intended to publish it separately and to alter it considerably, and the altered MS. was sent to Mr. Dallas for translation. This is so common a practice that it never occurred to me to state that the article had been modified; but now I much regret that I did not do so. The original will soon appear in German, and I believe will be a much larger book than the English one; for, with Dr. Krause's consent, many long extracts from Miss Seward were omitted (as well as much other matter) from being in my opinion superfluous for the English reader. I believe that the omitted parts will appear as notes in the German edition. Should there be a reprint of the English Life, I will state that the original as it appeared in *Kosmos* was modified by Dr. Krause before it was translated. I may add that I had obtained Dr. Krause's consent for a translation, and had arranged with Mr. Dallas before your book was announced. I remember this because Mr. Dallas wrote to tell me of the advertisement.—I remain, Yours faithfully, C. DARWIN.

Butler was not satisfied with this reply, and wrote to the *Athenæum*, 31st January, 1880. His letter recapitulates some of the facts which have just been set forth, but since something turns on the tone of it, I give it in full, with apologies for the repetition. I have, however, omitted the postscript, which comments on reviews of *Erasmus Darwin* and of *Evolution Old and New* and, for our present purpose, does not materially add to the letter.

S. Butler to the Editor of the Athenæum

EVOLUTION OLD AND NEW

I beg leave to lay before you the following facts:—

On February 22, 1879, my book *Evolution Old and New* was announced. It was published May 3, 1879. It contained a comparison of the theory of evolution as propounded by Dr. Erasmus Darwin with that of his grandson, Mr. Charles Darwin, the preference being decidedly given to the earlier writer. It also contained other matter which I could not omit, but which I am afraid may have given some offence to Mr. Darwin and his friends.

In November, 1879, Mr. Charles Darwin's *Life of Erasmus Darwin* appeared. It is to the line which Mr. Darwin has taken in connexion with this volume that I wish to call attention.

Mr. Darwin states in his preface that he is giving to the public a translation of an article by Dr. Krause, which appeared "in the February number of a well-known German scientific journal, *Kosmos*," then just entered on its second year. He adds in a note that the translator's "scientific reputation, together with his knowledge of German, is a guarantee for its accuracy." This is equivalent, I imagine, to guaranteeing the accuracy himself.

In a second note, upon the following page, he says that my work *Evolution Old and New* "has appeared since the publication of Dr. Krause's article." He thus distinctly precludes his readers from supposing that any passage they may meet with could have been written by the light of, or with reference to, my book.

On reading the English translation I found in it one point which appeared to have been taken from *Evolution Old and New*, and another which clearly and indisputably was so; I also found more than one paragraph, but especially the last—and perhaps most prominent in the book, as making the impression it was most desired the reader should carry away with him—which it was hard to believe was not written at myself; but I found no acknowledgment of what seemed taken from *Evolution Old and New*, nor any express reference to it.

In the face of the English translation itself, it was incredible that the writer had written without my work before him; in the face of the preface it was no less incredible that Mr. Darwin should have distinctly told his readers that he was giving them one article, when he must have perfectly well known that he was giving them another and very different one.

I therefore sent for the February number of *Kosmos* and compared the original with what purported to be the translation. I found many passages of the German omitted, and many in the English article were wholly wanting in the German. Among these latter were the passages I had conceived to be taken from me and the ones which were most adverse to me.

Dr. Krause's article begins on p. 131 of Mr. Darwin's book. There is new matter on pp. 132, 133, 134, 135, 136, 137, 138, 139, while almost the whole of pp. 147–152 inclusive, and all the last six pages are not to be found in the supposed original.

I then wrote to Mr. Darwin, putting the facts before him as they appeared to myself, and asking for an explanation; I received answer that Dr. Krause's article had been altered since publication, and that the altered MS. had been sent for translation. "This is so common a practice," writes Mr. Darwin, with that "happy simplicity" of which the *Pall Mall Gazette* (December 12th, 1879) declares him "to be a master," "that it never occurred to me to state that the article had been modified; but now I much regret that I did not do so." Mr. Darwin further says that, should there be a reprint of the English life of Dr. Darwin, he will state that the original as it appeared in *Kosmos* was modified by Dr. Krause. He does not, however, either deny or admit that the modification of the article was made by the light of, and with a view to, my book.

It is doubtless a common practice for writers to take an opportunity of revising their works, but it is not common when a covert condemnation of an opponent has been interpolated into a revised edition, the revision of which has been concealed, to declare with every circumstance of distinctness that the condemnation was written prior to the book which might appear to have called it forth, and thus lead readers to suppose that it must be an unbiassed opinion.

S. Butler

On reading this letter in the *Athenæum*, Charles Darwin looked up his papers and found that when he wrote to Butler, 3rd January, he had forgotten something. His instinct was to write to the *Athenæum*, and explain what had happened, but his intention was not carried into effect. He prepared two letters, the drafts of which are among the papers sent me by Mr. F. Darwin.[114]

PROPOSED LETTER NO. I

Charles Darwin to the Editor of the Athenæum.

Down, Beckenham, January 24th 80

Sir,—Mr. Butler in his letter in your last number seems to think me guilty of intentional duplicity in not having stated in the preface to my notice of the life of Erasmas Darwin, that Dr. Krause had considerably altered the article in *Kosmos* before he sent it to Mr. Dallas for translation. In my private letter to Mr. Butler I said that it was so common a practice for an author to alter an article before its republication, that it never occurred to me to state that this had been done in the present case. Afterwards a dim recollection crossed my mind that I had written something on the subject, and I looked at the first proof received from Messrs. Clowes and found in it the following passage, here copied verbatim:—

To the Compositor; Be so good as to insert inverted commas to the whole of this extract:—

"Dr. Krause has taken great pains, and has added largely to his essay as it appeared in *Kosmos*; and my preliminary notice, having

---

[114] [See Letter A, p. 168, Charles Darwin to his daughter Henrietta Litchfield.]

been written before I had seen the additions, unfortunately contains much repetition of what Dr. Krause has said. In fact, the present volume contains two distinct biographies, of which I have no doubt that by Dr. Krause is much the best. I have left it almost wholly to him to treat of what Dr. Darwin has done in science, more especially in regard to evolution."

The proof sheet was sent to Dr. Krause, with a letter in which I said that on further reflection it seemed to me absurd to publish two accounts of the life of the same man in the same volume; and that as my Notice was drawn up chiefly from unpublished documents, it appeared to me best that my account alone of the life should appear in England, with his account of the scientific works of Erasmus Darwin, but that he could, of course, publish the extracts from Miss Seward, etc., in the German edition. Dr. Krause, with the liberality and kindness which has characterised all his conduct towards me, agreed instantly to my suggestion; but added that he thought it better that the text of the German edition should correspond with the English one, and that he would add the extracts, etc., in a supplement or in footnotes. He then expressly asked me to strike out the passage above quoted, which I did; and having done so, it did not occur to me to add, as I ought to have done, that the retained parts of Dr. Krause's article had been much modified. It seems to me that anyone on comparing the article in *Kosmos* with the translation, and on finding many passages at the beginning omitted, and many towards the end added, might have inferred that the author had enlarged and improved it, without suspecting a deep scheme of duplicity. Finally, I may state, as I did in my letter to Mr. Butler, that I obtained Dr. Krause's permission for a translation of his article to appear in England, and Mr. Dallas agreed to translate it, before I heard of any announcement of Mr. Butler's last book.

He is mistaken in supposing that I was offended by this book, for I looked only at the part about the life of Erasmus Darwin; I did not even look at the part about evolution; for I had found in his former work that I could not make his views harmonize with what I knew. I was, indeed, told that this part contained some bitter sarcasms against me; but this determined me all the more not to read it.

As Mr. Butler evidently does not believe my deliberate assertion that the omission of any statement that Dr. Krause had altered his article before sending it for translation, was unintentional or accidental I think that I shall be justified in declining to answer any future attack which Mr. Butler may make on me.— Sir, Your obedient servant,

CHARLES DARWIN

The sentence "He is mistaken . . . not to read it" is marked as having been objected to, and there is a note showing that the whole letter was disapproved of by all Mr. Darwin's family. I cannot explain why this proposed letter is dated 24th January, 1880.[115] Butler's letter certainly did not appear till 31st January. It is possible it may have been ready for and crowded out of the preceding number of the *Athenæum* (24th January), and that Darwin had seen it in proof, but this seems unlikely. Nothing, however, turns upon the point.[116]

The foregoing letter being "disapproved by everyone" the draft of a second was prepared:—

[115]The covering letter to Mrs. Litchfield is clearly dated February 1st in the original. The date on the draft of Letter No. I in Cambridge University Library looks as though it had been added later. Possibly reference to a calendar after the letter had been written led to the mistake of exactly one week.—N. B.]

[116]Here follow Letters B, C, and D from R. B. Litchfield and Henrietta Litchfield, see pp. 169, 170, 173.]

PROPOSED LETTER NO. II

Charles Darwin to the Editor of the Athenæum
Down, Beckenham, Kent, February 1st, 1880

EVOLUTION OLD AND NEW

Sir,—In regard to the letter from Mr. Butler which appeared in your columns last week under the above heading, I wish to state that the omission of any mention of the alterations made by Dr. Krause in his article before it was re-published had no connection whatever with Mr. Butler. I find in the first proofs received from Messrs. Clowes the words: "Dr. Krause had added largely to his essay as it appeared in *Kosmos.*" These words were afterwards accidentally omitted, and when I wrote privately to Mr. Butler I had forgotten that they had ever been written. (I could explain distinctly how the accident arose, but the explanation does not seem to me worth giving.)[117] This omission, as I have already said, I much regret. It is a mere illusion on the part of Mr. Butler to suppose that it could make any difference to me whether or not the public knew that Dr. Krause's article had been added to or altered before being translated. The additions were made quite independently of any suggestion or wish on my part.

(As Mr. Butler evidently does not believe my deliberate assertion that the above omission was unintentional, I must decline any further discussion with him)[118]—

Sir, Your obedient servant, CHARLES DARWIN

This letter did not meet with the approval of all the Darwin family, and it was decided that it should be submitted to Professor Huxley for his opinion.[119]

[117] Bracketed in original by C. D.
[118] Bracketed in original by C. D.
[119] [See Letters E, F, G, H, pp. 174, 175, from R. B. Litchfield and C. Darwin].

Charles Darwin to T. H. Huxley
Down, Beckenham, Kent, February 2nd, 1880

My dear Huxley,—I am going to ask you to [do] me a great kindness. Mr. Butler has attacked me bitterly, in fact, accusing me of lying, duplicity, and God knows what, because I unintentionally omitted to state that Krause had enlarged his *Kosmos* article before sending it for translation. I have written the enclosed letter [Proposed letter No. II] to the *Athenæum*, but Litchfield [Mr. Darwin's son-in-law] is strongly opposed to my making any answer, and I enclose his letter, if you can find time to read it. Of the other members of my family, some are for and some against answering. I should rather like to show that I had intended to state that Krause had enlarged his article. On the other hand a clever and unscrupulous man like Mr. Butler would be sure to twist whatever I may say against me; and the longer the controversy lasts the more degrading it is to me. If my letter is printed, both the Litchfields want me to omit the two sentences now marked by pencil brackets, but I see no reason for the omission.

Now will you do me the lasting kindness to read carefully the attack and my answer, and as I have unbounded confidence in your judgment whatever you advise that I will do: whether you advise me to make no answer or to send the enclosed letter as it stands, or to strike out the sentences between the brackets?—

Ever yours sincerely, CHARLES DARWIN

P.S.—Since writing the above I have received another letter from Litchfield with a splendid imaginary letter from Butler, showing how he probably would travesty my answer. He tells me that he took the *Athenæum* to Mr. P[ollock] and asked him (without giving any hint of his own opinion) whether Butler's attack ought to be answered, and he said "No." But I wait in anxiety for your answer *as this will decide me.*

The two sentences marked by pencil brackets are "I could explain . . . worth giving," and "As Mr. Butler . . . with him." Professor Huxley's opinion was that the letter should not be sent; he thought that a note in a future edition of *Erasmus Darwin* would meet the case. Letter No. II was accordingly rejected.[120]

It appears from the papers sent me by Mr. F. Darwin that something else weighed with Charles Darwin and his advisers besides Professor Huxley's opinion, namely, that Butler's letter to the *Athenæum*, was "so ungentlemanlike as not to deserve an answer," as to which the reader has the material for forming his own opinion.

> *Charles Darwin to T. H. Huxley*
>   *Down, Beckenham, Kent, Feb.* 4 [1880]

My dear Huxley,—Oh Lord what a relief your letter has been to me. I feel like a man condemned to be hung who has just got a reprieve. I saw in the future no end of trouble, but I feared that I was bound in honour to answer. If you were here I would show you exactly how the omission arose. . . . You have indeed done me a lasting kindness.
—Yours affectionately, CH. DARWIN.

The affair has annoyed and pained me to a silly extent; but it would be disagreeable to anyone to be publicly called in fact a liar. He seems to hint that I interpolated sentences in Krause's MS., but he could hardly have really thought so. Until quite recently he expressed great friendship for me, and said he had learnt all he knew about evolution from my books, and I have no idea what has made him so bitter against me. You have done me a great kindness.

[120] [See Huxley's answer, Letter I. p. 176.]

Mr. Francis Darwin and some of his brothers disagreed with Huxley, and thought that their father ought to write. It is, of course, idle to say so now, but I wish Darwin had followed his son's advice and neglected that of Huxley. Butler would not have had to strain any point to accept his statement that he had written the words, and that they had been struck out inadvertently. He would not, and could not have twisted it against him, though he might have had something to say about his not believing the "deliberate assertion that the omission of any statement that Dr. Krause had altered his article before sending it for translation was unintentional or accidental," because he found no such "deliberate assertion" in Darwin's letter to him of 3rd January, 1880. What he found there was an assertion that to alter an article on republication is so common a practice that it never occurred to Darwin to mention it. He took this to mean that Darwin had done what he did on purpose. He would have had to know more than he was told in the letter of 3rd January, 1880, before he could have understood in what way the words "unintentional" and "accidental" could be properly applied to what had happened. We can now see that the inadvertence consisted in Darwin's not noticing that he was striking out of his preface more than he intended. So long as the words stating that Dr. Krause had altered his article between February and November were there, all was well; the first footnote guaranteed the accuracy of the translation of the *modified article*, and the second footnote explained how it had been possible for Dr. Krause to make the modifications with Butler's book before him. But when the words were struck out, the unforeseen result followed that the meaning of both the footnotes became altered. The first footnote about Mr. Dallas now referred to the *unmodified article*, and practically declared that it had been translated as it originally appeared in *Kosmos*; and the second note, that *Evolution Old and New* had appeared since *Kosmos*, confirmed this meaning by implying particularly that noth-

ing in the translated article could possibly have got there in consequence of *Evolution Old and New*.

In 1880 Butler published *Unconscious Memory*, wherein he told
the story over again, and very fully. The reader may perhaps ask:
Why should he do so? What could it matter to him? How was he
damnified by what had been done? And it may be conceded that
if he had issued a writ claiming damages and Darwin had paid
into Court one shilling, no jury would have awarded him more.
But Butler was not thinking of shillings or pounds. He shows in
Chapter IV of *Unconscious Memory* that the personal damage he
considered himself to have sustained consisted in Darwin's having
made it appear that if anything condemnatory of *Evolution Old and
New* was to be found in Dr. Krause's translated article, "it was an
undesigned coincidence and would show how little worthy I must
be to consideration when my opinions were refuted in advance by
one who could have no bias in regard to them." Later in the chapter, he writes as follows:—

By far the most important notice of *Evolution Old and New* was
that taken by Mr. Darwin himself; for I can hardly be mistaken in
believing that Dr. Krause's article would have been allowed to
repose unaltered in the pages of the well-known German scientific journal, *Kosmos*, unless something had happened to make Mr.
Darwin feel that his reticence concerning his grandfather must
now be ended. . . .

This (Darwin's letter of 3rd January, 1880) was not a letter I
could accept. If Mr. Darwin had said that by some inadvertence,
which he was unable to excuse or account for, a blunder had been
made which he would at once correct so far as was in his power by
a letter to the *Times* or the *Athenæum*, and that a notice of the erratum should be printed on a fly-leaf and pasted into all unsold
copies of the *Life of Erasmus Darwin*, there would have been no
more heard of the matter from me; but when Mr. Darwin main-

tained that it was a common practice to take advantage of an opportunity of revising a work to interpolate a covert attack upon an opponent, and at the same time to misdate the interpolated matter by expressly stating that it appeared months sooner than it actually did, and prior to the work which it attacked; when he maintained that what was being done was "so common a practice that it never occurred" to him—the writer of some twenty volumes—to do what all literary men must know to be inexorably requisite, I thought this was going far beyond what was permissible in honourable warfare, and that it was time, in the interests of literary and scientific morality, even more than in my own, to appeal to public opinion.

In developing this subject Butler uses the personal quarrel as an occasion for referring to Charles Darwin's treatment of Buffon, Erasmus Darwin, Lamarck, and the author of *The Vestiges of Creation*, in order to show that his indignation was aroused on behalf of these writers, "to all of whom," he considered, "Mr. Darwin had dealt the same measure which he was now dealing to myself." It is necessary just to mention this, lest it should be thought that Butler was complaining selfishly, but to say more would be to raise a question that is fully discussed from Butler's point of view in *Evolution Old and New*, and to neglect the personal quarrel with which alone we are now concerned.

When *Unconscious Memory* was published, the question arose as to what was to be done with regard to Butler's repetition of his accusation, and again there was disagreement among the members of the Darwin family. Mr. Francis Darwin and some of his brothers wished "that a fly-sheet should be inserted in the unsold copies of the *Life of Erasmus Darwin*, stating as an erratum on p. 1, 10 lines from top, that Krause's article in *Kosmos* was altered and enlarged before it was sent to Mr. Dallas for translation." The other members of the family did not agree, and *Unconscious Memory* was sent to Mr.

(afterwards Sir) Leslie Stephen for his opinion. He advised that nothing should be done, and this advice was adopted.[121]

On the 19th April, 1882, Charles Darwin died. Butler was at the time bringing out a new edition of *Evolution Old and New*, with an Appendix consisting of two chapters of which the first was about the reviews of the first edition, and contained this sentence:—

The way in which Mr. Charles Darwin met *Evolution Old and New* has been so fully dealt with in my book *Unconscious Memory*; in the *Athenæum,* Jan. 31, 1880; the *St. James's Gazette*, Dec. 8, 1880; and *Nature*, Feb. 3, 1881, that I need not return to it here, more especially as Mr. Darwin has, by his silence, admitted that he has no defence to make.

This is the preface to the second edition of *Evolution Old and New*, it is dated 21st April, 1882:—

Since the proof sheets of the Appendix to this book left my hands, finally corrected, and too late for me to be able to re-cast the first of the two chapters that compose it, I hear, with the most profound regret, of the death of Mr. Charles Darwin.

It being still possible for me to refer to this event in a preface, I hasten to say how much it grates upon me to appear to renew my attack upon Mr. Darwin under present circumstances.

I have insisted in each of my three books on Evolution upon the immensity of the service which Mr. Darwin rendered to that transcendently important theory. In *Life and Habit* I said: "To the end of time, if the question be asked, 'Who taught people to believe in Evolution?' the answer must be that it was Mr. Darwin." This is true; and it is hard to see what palm of higher praise can be awarded to any philosopher.

[121] [Letters J & K pp. 177, 178, from H. Litchfield to Leslie Stephen and his reply.]

I have always admitted myself to be under the deepest obligations to Mr. Darwin's works; and it was with the greatest reluctance, not to say repugnance, that I became one of his opponents. I have partaken of his hospitality, and have had too much experience of the charming simplicity of his manner not to be among the readiest to at once admire and envy it. It is unfortunately true that I believe Mr. Darwin to have behaved badly to me; this is too notorious to be denied; but at the same time I cannot be blind to the fact that no man can be judge in his own case, and that, after all, Mr. Darwin may have been right and I wrong.

At the present moment, let me impress this latter alternative upon my mind as far as possible, and dwell only upon that side of Mr. Darwin's work and character about which there is no difference of opinion among either his admirers or his opponents.[122]

Butler ought perhaps to have sent a copy of this book to Mr. Francis Darwin. He did not do so, I suppose, because he shrank from intruding upon him with his own affairs at such a moment; and no doubt he also trusted to its coming to his notice in the ordinary course. But Mr. Francis Darwin did not see the book, and knew nothing about this preface till I read it to him in November, 1910.

At the end of 1887 Mr. Francis Darwin published *The Life and Letters of Charles Darwin*. It contains this passage, III, 220:—

The publication of the *Life of Erasmus Darwin* led to an attack by Mr. Samuel Butler, which amounted to a charge of falsehood against my father. After consulting his friends, he came to the determination to leave the charge unanswered, as being unworthy of his notice. (*Footnote by Mr. F. Darwin*: He had, in a letter to Mr. Butler, expressed his regret at the oversight which caused so much offence.) Those who wish to know more of the matter, may gather the facts of the case from Ernst Krause's *Charles Darwin*, and they will find Mr. Butler's statement of his grievance in the *Athenæum*, January 31, 1880, and in the *St. James's Gazette*, December 8, 1880. The affair gave my father much pain, but the warm sympathy of those whose opinion he respected soon helped him to let it pass into a well-merited oblivion.

On this, Butler wrote to the *Athenæum*, 26th November, 1887, reiterating his accusation and complaining that Charles Darwin had taken no step towards a public correction of his mis-statement.

About the same time Mr. Francis Darwin published a new edition of *Erasmus Darwin*, and fulfilled his father's promise to Butler by adding to the preface a third footnote:—

Mr. Darwin accidentally omitted to mention that Dr. Krause revised, and made certain alterations to, his Essay before it was translated. Among these additions is an allusion to Mr. Butler's book *Evolution Old and New*.

Butler saw that this third footnote changed the sense which the other two footnotes had borne when they stood alone in the preface to the first edition, and wrote to the *Academy*, 17th December, 1887: "Mr. Francis Darwin has now stultified his father's preface." In so writing he did not know, and he had no means of knowing, that Mr. Francis Darwin's third footnote had restored to the preface the meaning which Charles Darwin had originally intended it to bear.

Butler noted several public allusions to *Life and Habit* by Mr. Francis Darwin. Here are two of such allusions. At the Cardiff Meeting of the British Association in 1891, Mr. F. Darwin read a paper, published in the *Annals of Botany* (VI, 1892), *On the Artificial Production of Rhythm in Plants*, by Francis Darwin and Dorothea F. M. Pertz, in which the following sentence occurs: "This repeating power may be that fundamental property of living matter which stretches from inheritance on one side to memory on the other (see Mr. Samuel Butler's *Life and Habit*)."

In 1901 Mr. F. Darwin delivered a lecture at the Glasgow Meeting of the British Association *On the Movements of Plants*. The report in *Nature*, 14th November, 1901, contains this sentence: "If we take the wide view of memory which has been set forth by Mr. S. Butler (*Life and Habit*, 1878) and by Professor Hering, we shall be forced to believe that plants, like all other living things, have a kind of memory."

Butler died on the 18th June, 1902.[123]

In 1908, when President of the British Association, in his Inaugural Address at Dublin, Mr. Francis Darwin paid Butler the posthumous honour of quoting from his translation of Hering's lecture *On Memory* which is in *Unconscious Memory*, and of mentioning Butler as having independently arrived at a theory similar to Hering's. (See the report in *Nature*, 3rd September, 1908.)

It is partly because of these public allusions to *Life and Habit*, by Mr. F. Darwin, that Butler is now more considered than he was formerly, and that it is being understood at last how serious a purpose underlies his humour.

In May, 1910, Mr. Streatfeild, as Butler's literary executor, published a new edition of *Unconscious Memory* with an introduction by Professor Marcus Hartog, summarising Butler's views on biology, and defining his position in the world of science. It seemed a fortunate moment for this reprint to appear, first, because of Mr. Francis Darwin's Presidential Address; secondly, because many sheets of the original edition of the book had been destroyed in a fire at Ballantyne's some years before, so that anyone who might have wanted to refer to Hering's address would be unable to obtain Butler's translation of it; and, thirdly, because of the changed views of scientific men in regard to biology, and what is called "Darwinism."

---

[123] [Letter L, p. 181 from Francis Darwin to Henrietta Litchfield].

In June, 1910, Mr. Francis Darwin put himself into communication with me, and sent me the letters as I have said above. If he had sent them before, instead of after the new edition of *Unconscious Memory* was published, Mr. Streatfeild would have included the substance of these pages as a note or addendum to that book, for it is there that these facts ought to be recorded. In the course of our correspondence I asked Mr. F. Darwin whether he consented to my making public the fact that he and some of his brothers disapproved of the advice given by Huxley and Leslie Stephen; at the same time I inquired whether he had had any other special reason for sending me the papers. He gave his consent, and added: "I had hoped that the general impression of the papers sent you would have led you to suspect that Butler was mistaken, but I do not mean to complain if this is not in any degree the case."

I understood him to mean mistaken in supposing that Mr. Darwin had undertaken his book *Erasmus Darwin* because of or with reference to *Evolution Old and New*. Even in 1879–80, when the events were proceeding, I had suspected that Butler might have been mistaken in this, and I, therefore, told Mr. F. Darwin so. I could not tell him that my suspicion arose in consequence of reading the letters he sent me, but I may now say that on reading them, and thinking them over again, I have become convinced that Butler must have been mistaken. Further, I am sure that if he had known what we know now he would have been confirmed in what he wrote in his preface to the second edition of *Evolution Old and New*, that Charles Darwin may have been right and he wrong, and would have taken or made an opportunity of putting the matter straight.

The case then stood thus: Butler's accusation was in three counts:—

(1) That Charles Darwin undertook *Erasmus Darwin* because of or with reference to *Evolution Old and New*;

(2) That his preface contained an error;

(3) That he made a mistake in the line he took when the error was pointed out to him.

Mr. F. Darwin admitted (3) by saying that he disapproved of the way in which the matter was treated; I gave up (1) by admitting that Butler must have been mistaken; and we agreed about (2).

Having reached this point, Mr. F. Darwin wrote in a subsequent letter: "I have often regretted that when the quarrel began I did not go to Butler and have it out *viva voce*. I also think I was mistaken in not publishing in *Life and Letters* a full account of the thing." This reminded me of something in Butler's note-books, viz. an account of how a lady, whom Butler knew, met Mr. Francis Darwin at Cambridge, in 1894, and they spoke about the quarrel, Mr. F. Darwin saying to her much the same as he wrote to me. The lady repeated the conversation to Butler, and he derived the impression that Mr. F. Darwin regretted the incident, and would be glad to arrive at a reconciliation. But remembering his preface to the second edition of *Evolution Old and New*, and assuming that Mr. F. Darwin had seen it, he felt that it was impossible for him to make any further move, and though he would have welcomed any public move from the other side, none was made, and nothing happened. This note showed me that I had treated the opportunity given me by Mr. F. Darwin in the spirit in which Butler himself would have treated it if it had been offered to him.

Darwin and Butler cannot now meet and adjust their differences; nevertheless, unknown to themselves they have met and parted and met again in the correspondence that has taken place between Mr. Francis Darwin and myself; I trust we have succeeded in composing their quarrel in so far as it may be given to the representatives of dead men to act for them. All the time there has been running in my head the sonnet about immortality which Butler wrote in 1898, for I know that, though he was thinking of immortality in a broad sense, he had not forgotten his dispute with Charles Darwin, whose pupil he had been, and whom he also held as foe.

Μέλλουτα ταῦτα

Not on sad Stygian shore, nor in clear sheen
Of far Elysian plain, shall we meet those
Among the dead whose pupils we have been,
Nor those great shades whom we have held as foes;
No meadow of asphodel our feet shall tread,
Nor shall we look each other in the face
To love or hate each other, being dead,
Hoping some praise, or fearing some disgrace.
We shall not argue, saying "'Twas thus" or "Thus,"
Our argument's whole drift we shall forget;
Who's right, who's wrong, 'twill be all one to us;
We shall not even know that we have met.
　　Yet meet we shall and part and meet again
　　Where dead men meet, on lips of living men.

[Here ends Festing Jones's Pamphlet]

The letters which follow from the Cambridge University
Library, fill in gaps in the already complicated structure of the
Pamphlet. Page cross-references will show where they should be
inserted chronologically. I will begin, however, by quoting three
letters from Samuel Butler written before the quarrel,[124] when he
was still a whole-hearted humble admirer of Charles Darwin.
Resentment had not then warped his saner judgment.

　　　　　　　　　　　　　　15 *Clifford's Inn, Oct. 1st* 1865
Dear Sir,
　　. . . . . . My *study* is art, and anything else I may indulge in is
only by-play; . . . .

---

[124] Printed in Henry Festing Jones's *Samuel Butler A Memoir*, Macmillan & Co.,
1919, Vol. I. p. 123, 156 and 189.

I always delighted in your origin of species as soon as I saw it out in New Zealand,—not as knowing anything whatsoever of natural history, but it enters into so many deeply interesting questions, or rather it suggests so many that it thoroughly fascinated me. . . .

Six years later Butler published *Erewhon* and some critics believed that it formed an attack on the *Origin of Species*; hence the disclaimer in this letter.

15 *Clifford's Inn, May* 11 1872

Dear Sir,

I venture upon the liberty of writing to you about a portion of the little book *Erewhon* which I have lately published and which I am afraid has been a good deal misunderstood. I refer to the chapter on Machines in which I have developed and worked out the obviously absurd theory that they are about to supplant the human race and be developed into a higher kind of life.

When I first got hold of the idea I developed it for mere fun, and because it amused me and I thought it would amuse others, but without a particle of serious meaning; but I developed it and introduced (it) into *Erewhon* with the intention of implying "See how easy it is to be plausible, and what absurd propositions can be defended by a little ingenuity and distortion and departure from strictly scientific methods," and I had Butler's *Analogy* in my head as the book at which it should be aimed, but preferred to conceal my aim for many reasons. Firstly the book was already as heavily weighted with heterodoxy as it would bear, and I dare not give another half ounce lest it should break the camel's back; secondly it would have interfered with the plausibility of the argument, and I looked to this plausibility as a valuable aid to the general acceptation of the book: thirdly it is more amusing without any sort of explanation, and I thought the drier part that had gone before wanted a little relieving; also the more enigmatic a thing of this sort is, the more people think for themselves about it, on the principle that advertisers ask "Where is Eliza?" and "Who's Griffiths?" I therefore thought it unnecessary to give any disclaimer of an intention of being disrespectful to the *Origin of Species* a book for which I can never be sufficiently grateful, though I am well aware how utterly incapable I am of forming any opinion on a scientific subject which is worth a moment's consideration.

However you have a position which nothing can shake and I know very well that any appearance of ridicule would do your theories no harm whatever, and that they could afford a far more serious satire than anything in *Erewhon*—the only question was how far *I* could afford to be misrepresented as disbelieving in things which I believe most firmly. . . . I am sincerely sorry that some of the critics should have thought that I was laughing at your theory, a thing which I never meant to do, and should be shocked at having done.

I am Sir, Yours respectfully,

S. BUTLER

Even in 1873 friendly intercourse still continued. *The Fair Haven* had been published, and Darwin had written an appreciative letter. Butler's mother had died, and her death coinciding with the publication of *The Fair Haven* with its anti-religious implications, gave Butler an acute sense of guilt.

Clifford's Inn, 15/4/73

Dear Mr. Darwin,

Your very kind letter concerning *The Fair Haven* was forwarded to me at Mentone from which place I returned on Sunday morning early. You will doubtless have seen the cause of my journey in *The Times* obituary list.

Had I known how ill my poor mother was I could not have brought out or even written my book at such a time, but her recovery was confidently expected till within a fortnight of her death, and it was not until I actually arrived at Mentone that I knew *how* long she must have been ill and suffering. I must own that I feel that there is something peculiarly unsuitable in the time of my book's appearing but it was actually published before I was aware of the circumstances. I am thankful that she can never know. Of course it remains to be seen what the verdict of the public will be but I am greatly encouraged by the letters received from yourself and Mr. Stephen . . . I shall try a novel pure and simple with little "purpose" next, but it remains to be seen whether I can do it. I would say that I have no "purpose" in my novel at all, but I am still in the flesh and however much the spirit may be willing I fear that the cloven hoof will show itself ever and anon. . . .

Again thanking you very sincerely for all the kindness you have shown me, with kind regards to Mrs. Darwin,

Yours very truly

S. BUTLER

The following sequence of letters form the unpublished background of doubt and indecision caused by the events described in the Festing Jones Pamphlet, pp. 135–164.

Charles Darwin sent the draft of Proposed letter No. I—his first suggested answer to S. Butler—with the following covering Letter A to his daughter, Mrs. Litchfield. The family at Down seem to have wavered about an answer. On January 26 1880, Emma (Mrs. Darwin) wrote to her son George who was abroad:—

"F [father] is a good deal bothered by S. Butler's attack which is expected in the *Athenæum*. He wrote a note to F [father] saying he was going to lay 'all the facts' before the public. We are all anxious that he should take no notice of it."

LETTER A, SEE P. 149

Charles Darwin to Henrietta Litchfield

Feb. 1, 1880. Down, Beckenham, Kent

My dear Henrietta,

Will you and Litchfield read article in *Athenæum* and my answer.—I have resolved to send one, as I can say something in defence of my negligence.—I wish my letter to appear in next number and I should like to see proof, so if you do not object to anything greatly please post it on Monday addressed to Editor of *Athenæum with my note to Editor*; and return the *Athenæum* to me.

If you or Litchfield object very strongly to anything, please return my letter here that I may post it on Tuesday. The *Athenæum* is published on Friday evening. There is one sentence of which Frank suggested the insertion; but I am doubtful and so is your Mother.—It is on separate paper, and if inserted please gum it in by cutting p. 3 in two pieces before the last paragraph, beginning with words "As Mr. Butler evidently does not believe etc."

It is very disagreeable being accused of duplicity and falsehood. All here approve of letter.

Since the above was written I have by advice of Frank and Leonard re-written my letter and shortened it. I hope that you and L[itchfield] may approve of it. If you do not I cannot promise to follow your advice, but it shall be well considered.

I am sure that neither of you will grudge the bother of considering the case.—Mr. Butler's letter is very artful: he throughout makes it appear as if I had written Dr. Krause's part.

Yours affectionately, C. DARWIN

There follow the answers of R. B. Litchfield, Darwin's son-in-law and Henrietta, Darwin's daughter, disapproving of draft answer No. I.

LETTER B, SEE P. 151

R. B. Litchfield to Charles Darwin

Feb. 1 [1880]   4, *Bryanston St., Portman Sq., W.*

Dear Mr. Darwin,

Henrietta asks me to write my ideas on the Butler letter and your proposed answer.

When I read Butler's statement at the Club yesterday I was much relieved to find it was of a kind which, as I thought, made *any answer* absolutely unnecessary. Neither in form, nor in substance, is it such as to suggest that a reply is expected. You will discern that it does not, in common with newspaper attacks, ask for any further information or explanation, or touch any point of fact on which either the assailant, or a reader, could require such. In short, I never was clearer about anything than that, if it were my case, I should say nothing.

I tried, a second time, to read the statement, as if I were an outsider who knew nothing of the quarrel, and felt entirely sure this is the right conclusion.

Not one reader in a thousand will make head or tail of the grievance. It's all muddled up with complaints against divers reviewers.—This alone practically neutralizes any effect it might have had otherwise. Then if an attentive reader *does* care to look back and see what the complaint was he will also see (though in a brief form) your substantial reply; and this is, on the face of it, sufficient for the purpose. All the rest of B's insinuations read to an outsider as merely the annoyance and venom of a man out of temper and hitting wildly about him.

If you answer him you bring about *exactly* the result he most wants, wh is to fill people's heads with the notion that yr book is in some way a reply or rejoinder to his: in fact you make it a "Darwin-Butler affaire" as the French wd say—and this is what will delight him.

As it stands there is nothing wh any friend of yors or any absolutely indifferent person cd want explained or answered, and the *tone* of Butler is of itself quite enough to deprive him of any shadow of *claim* to an answer wh a loyal or friendly correspondent might have.

What I am trying to convey in this letter is that I have thought the thing over as a *cold outsider*, and that it is in this character that I am against replying to B.

I agree however wholly with all that H. says as to yr draft reply. Yrs affec R. B. L.

LETTER C, SEE P. 151

4, *Bryanston St., Portman Sq., W.*   *Feb.* 1, 1880
Dear Mr. Darwin,

Since sending off our last packet I bethought myself I shd like to ask the first *bystander* I could meet how Butler's letter struck him as regards the need of an answer, and so I went in and shewed the *Athenm* to Pollock in this street. As an accustomed literary man and man of the world I wanted to see whether he wd agree w me.—But of course I did not tell him anything before he read the article. I merely said when you have read it I want to ask yr opinion on a certain point, and when he had read it my question was does that in yr opinion need any answer? His reply was 1st. that he *might* be prejudiced as he knew something of B.—but he was strong that it *didn't* want answering (of course I didn't lead him to suppose it was any more than a question *from me* personally).

He had himself written the Pall Mall Article as it happened—and also an art in Sat. Rev. on Butler's Book. B., he tells me, is known to be getting up a grand reply to all his critics and he is making a point of getting their names. He wrote to the Saty w this enquy but the Saty put him off with a formal refusal. All wh helps to shew that he is a virulent Salamander of a man who will fight to the end, and as P. said, his greatest joy wd be to get into a public dispute w a man of eminence.

P., however, tho' aware of his character, was by no means prejudiced agst his bks (he thinks them nonsense but very clever nonsense) and his opinion on the question of a reply was I have no doubt a dry opinion. I have since looked with a critical eye at yr draft and I am only confirmed in my impression, for I do not find that it, in substance, contains anything wh is not already in the sentence quoted by B. from yr note. But while to the *substance* of your explanation it adds nothing it gives B the most admirable chance for another nasty letter inasmuch as it gives him *new facts*. At present he knows, and need know, nothing of the mere mechanical detail of the accident wh caused the omission. These you in fact give him. As he is now he *cannot* say anything more! he has made the worst of all he knows. But to a wretched unscrupulous word-fencer as he is yr letter opens material for a wholly new attack, and if the Athm likes to put it in, he can easily make it appear that there's something very suspicious and mysterious in yr proceedings.

Given only that a man [that] is a blackguard and there is no end to the stuff he mightn't write on such a theme. For illustration's sake I have put down a few sentences, as they came into my head, such as he might string together.

The fact is that such a story as that of the alterations of the proofs in this case, *cannot* be made satisfactory unless it is told in full: and of course to tell it in full wd be ridiculous. The main topic is itself a merely microscopic point, and to go *into* the business wd be too intolerable.

But over and above all special considerations is the one that a reply in such a case is *necessarily* an apologetic process, and that you have *nothing to apologise for*.

I daresay much of this repeats Henrietta. In what she has read to me I wholly agree.

R. B. LITCHFIELD

Sketch of imaginary reply of Butler's. By R. B. Litchfield

Sir, When I wrote etc. last week I thought I knew all that was likely to be known abt Mr. Darwin's extraordinary treatment of my book, but his letter to you makes some most remarkable additions to the strange story. Mr. D. had told me that it "never occurred to him" to state etc. Never occurred to him!! When now it seems that it not only occurred to him, but that he *did* state etc. etc. Stated it in a printed preface, and afterwards, in some mysterious way, this statement disappeared from the proof! Perhaps Mr. D. will complete the story etc. etc. Sentences do not vanish out of a printed page by accident *only*, etc. etc. He goes on to tell us that "it is an illusion to suppose it cd make any diffce" etc. etc. It *might* have been an illusion due to my ignorance but the details kindly given by Mr. D. now shew it to be a fact that it *did* make a difference. If no diffce why was the sentence expunged? If the excision was an accident it is of course needless for Mr. D. to tell us that it had nothing to do with Mr. Butler.—Accidents do not usually need to be thus explained, etc. etc. Nor is a great Naturalist the man we shd think likely wholly to forget! the act of cancelling his own deliberate statements.

Then Mr. D. tells us that the addns were made independently etc. Strange that an author of distinction shd be so delightfully pliable in the hands of somebody else. Who this somebody else might be, whether Dr. K. or etc. etc. we are not told. And lastly Mr. D. is obligg eno to say that I do not believe his delib assertion etc. I have not to my knowledge adopted this severe estimate of Mr. D.'s veracity, but certainly if Mr. D. wanted to create the incredulity wh he is so polite as to attribute to me the best means of achieving that result wd be to supply me with more of the explanations of wh he has given a sample in yr columns of Sty last.

LETTER D, UNDATED, SEE P. 151

LETTER D, UNDATED, SEE P. 151

Henrietta Litchfield to Charles Darwin

My dear Father,

R. was very late coming in so that we had rather a hurried consultation over the letter and I did not thank you for caring to consult us—which I do most heartily whatever you do with our advice. You will see by my first letter which was written before I got yours how sure I felt that you wd. not think of answering Butler.

I foresee one result of your letter that Butler will say you have been guilty of another quibble,—first you say to him that it never occurred to you to state that Krause had altered his article and then that you actually had it in the proof sheets and as you say accidentally omitted to publish it. Now Butler will say which of these two statements are true—and so it gives him scope for a whole set of fresh insults,—and with his clever pen he can make something very disagreeable out of this. The world will only know or at any rate remember that you and Butler had a controversy in which he will have the last word. If they understand it at all they'll see that its nothing whatever against you, but if they merely know that there have been letters backwards and forwards they may think there is some ground for Butler's accusation agst. you of jealousy of your grandfather.

If you leave the letter alone the facts are all there for those who care to read them, and it remains that Butler said some nasty spiteful things which you didn't care to answer. So Goodbye, dear Father—you get enough advice from us in quantity.

Your most affec., H. E. L.

The Litchfields' approval was again solicited on the question of submitting the question of a reply to T. H. Huxley.

LETTER E, SEE P. 152

R. B. Litchfield to Charles Darwin

3 *Feb.* 1880   4 *Bryanston St., Portman Sq., W.*
Dear Mr. Darwin,

I think Huxley's judgmt will be a safe one on the question of replyg to Butler—unless it be perhaps that he is himself horribly pugnacious and wd *naturally* be for fighting.

I still cannot frame to myself *any* answer wh wd be of the slightest use, or logically sound, except it confine itself to a mere reiteratn of what you've already told B. If such a reply seems any good it might be in such form as I have put down on back of this.

I *do* think it of the most supreme importance *not* to allude to B's pretending to think you untrustworthy—and that any reply shd be *absolutely* without feeling.

Always yrs affly, R. B. L.

LETTER F, SEE P. 152

On back of same sheet is Litchfield's suggested reply

EVOLUTION OLD AND NEW

Sir, I have read the statement by Mr. S. Butler wh appeared in yr columns of Saty last under the above heading, as to my having omitted to mention, in the preface to the lately issued translatn of Dr. Krause's essay on Erasmus Darwin, that his paper had been somewhat altered before being thus republished. As Mr. Butler quotes my letter to him in wh I informed him that this omission was accidental, and that it shd be corrected in case of the little book reaching a second edition, I do not see that I need trouble yr readers with any further observations on the matter.

LETTER G, SEE P. 152

Emma's comments to her son George, still abroad
(*In private possession*)

Down, Monday, Feb. 2, 1880

My dear George,

. . . We have been greatly excited by Butler's attack, w. appeared in the last *Ath*. F.[ather] wrote an answer to it and sent it up by John [the coachman] to shew it to R[ichard] and Hen[rietta]. John brought back a most sensible letter from R. giving all the reasons against taking any notice of it. R[ichard]'s letter is most excellent and makes me astonished that so sensible a man can talk such nonsense as he does sometimes. . . . It is an odious spiteful letter [Butler's to the *Athenæum*] but so tedious and confused in its accusations, that no indifft person will have patience to master it. As F[ather] had a stisfac. reply to make I was in favour of his sending it; but I have changed my opinion and F[ather] is going to send his reply and R[ichard]'s letter to Huxley and abide by his opinion. Certainly nothing w. please Butler so m. as an answer from F[ather] to which he cd. make a rejoinder and set up a Butler-Darwin controversy. F[ather] was much bothered at first but will now cast it off his mind.

LETTER H, SEE P. 152

Charles Darwin's reply to R. B. Litchfield

Feb. 2nd, 1880 [*Wrongly dated*]   *Down, Beckenham, Kent*
My dear Litchfield,

I have only a minute or two to thank you and Hen. *most warmly* for all the trouble which you have taken. Your first letter I think about the most sensible one I ever read. Your imaginary answer for B. is splendid! I am almost converted not to answer and I did not think I could be. Indeed I am converted—so almost is Mother—Leonard partially—F[rank] still maintains that if it were his case he would answer. We had thought of Huxley and I shall despatch by this post the *Athenæum* and my answer to him, and I will enclose (for I think you could not object) your first letter. I will not enclose 2nd letter, merely not to trouble H. with reading so much. I hope to God Huxley will say No. We do not agree about the 2 sentences to be cut out, if my answer is to be printed.

You have both been very very kind to me. The affair has pained me to a silly extent.

Yours affectionately, CH. DARWIN

LETTER I

Written on South Kensington Science and Art note-paper

T. H. Huxley to C. Darwin, in answer to the question should Darwin answer the attack of Samuel Butler's in the Athenæum. See p. 154 *Festing Jones Pamphlet.*

Feb. 3, 1880

My dear Darwin,

I read Butler's letter and your draft—and Litchfield's letter—last night; slept over them, and after lecturing about Dog-fish and Chimaera (subjects which have a distinct appropriateness to Butler) I have read them again.—And I say without the least hesitation, burn your draft and take no notice whatever of Mr. Butler until the next edition of your book comes out—when the briefest possible note explanatory of the circumstances—will be all that is necessary. Litchfield ought hereafter to be called 'the judicious' as Hooker was (I don't mean Sir Joe but the Divine); to my mind nothing can be sounder than his advice and "I am a man of (sor)rows and acquainted with (coming to) grief."

I am astounded at Butler—who I thought was a gentleman though his last book appeared to me to be supremely foolish.

Has Mivart bitten him and given him Darwinophobia?
Its a horrid disease and I would kill any

son of a

I found running loose with it without mercy. But don't you worry
with these things. Recollect what old Goethe said about his But-
lers and Mivarts:

> "Hat doch der Wallfisch seine Laus
> Muss auch die Meine haben."

We are as jolly as people can be who have been living in the dark
for a week and I hope you are all florishing. Ever yours, T. H. H.

Butler's attacks were repeated with renewed vigour when he
published *Unconscious Memory* later in 1880, and the peace of the
Darwin family was again disturbed. Early in 1881 outside advice
was once more sought.

LETTER J, SEE P. 158

Henrietta Litchfield to Leslie Stephen.

Jan. 1881 *2 Bryanston St., Portman Place*
Dear Mr. Stephen,
We have been having a great family talk and at last have come
to such a hopeless division of opinion that my Father has commis-
sioned me to write and ask you whether you wd. be so very kind
as to consider the following question and give him your judgment
as to what he had better do. . . .

The question is as to the advisability or necessity of his meeting in any way Butler's allegations that he has made a false statement in his preface to the *Life of Erasmus Darwin* which Butler considers does him great injury. . . .

The only point which some of us think my Father shd. meet is the alleged implication in the preface to the *Life of Eras. Darwin* that Krause's original article in *Kosmos* was not altered or added to before translation. . . .

Two or three of my brothers much wish that a fly leaf should be inserted in the unsold copies of the *Life of Erasmus D.* stating as an erratum on p. 1 10 lines from top that Krause's article in *Kosmos* was altered and enlarged before it was sent to Mr. Dallas for translation.

My husband and I are very strong on the other hand that nothing whatever should be done.

My brother Leonard will be the Devil's Advocate and will send you what he has to say. . . .

Henrietta Litchfield then states in three more pages her own and her husband's views.

LETTER K, SEE P. 158

Leslie Stephen to Charles Darwin

13 *Hyde Park Gate South, S.W.*

I return the books
by post.   12.1.80 [*Should be* 81]

My dear Mr. Darwin,

I hope that you will not object to my saying by way of preface to my answer to your question that it would always give me pride and pleasure if I could be of any service to you. I owe (like many more distinguished men) so great a debt to your writings that I should be glad to make the most trifling return: and I have (if

I may say so) that personal respect for you which every one must feel who knows you at all.

When you tell me that it pains you to be called a liar in your old age, I can quite understand it. To hear you called a liar makes me wish to give somebody such a slap in the face as he would have cause to remember. But I also reflect that you and your friends are bound also to remember your position and to avoid undignified squabbles. After all a man who insults you in that way is only exhibiting his own want of any claims to respect.

My opinion about the matter is perfectly distinct and unhesitating. I think that you should take no further notice of Mr. Butler whatever.

Perhaps it would be wiser to say nothing more: but I give you my reasons on another sheet, wh. you can read or put in the fire as you please.

Your book shall be put in the most honourable place in my library. When I have a chance of seeing you, I shall ask you to write my name as there are one or two little Stephens who may someday be pleased of any token of your esteem for their papa.

Yours very truly, L. STEPHEN

Leslie Stephen's reasons added on other sheets.

I think that Mr. Darwin should take no further notice of Mr. Butler. My reasons are as follows.

Butler has deprived himself of any claim to personal consideration by his want of common courtesy. Any injury done to him should of course be redressed. But he must not be taken as a judge of what constitutes an injury. Had he kept within the bounds of courtesy, it might have been proper to consider his fancies as well as his arguments. As he has exceeded those bounds so greatly, the only question is whether any wrong is being done to him. Now, in my opinion, there is no real injury whatever. If the inaccuracy in the preface injures anyone, it injures Mr. Darwin: for it takes no notice of the revision (and presumable improvement) of Krause's article. Every statement bearing upon Butler would remain absolutely unaffected whether it were or were not noticed in the preface. When I reprint articles from reviews, I revise them as a matter of course and without thinking myself bound to give any notice of the fact. The publication of Mr. Darwin's letter and the promise to introduce a change in future editions is, in my opinion, amply sufficient for any purpose. But in any case, Butler is not injured. He only comes in for a reference, not promised in the preface. This is, I think, the plainer from Butler's own chapter. He does not really even allege any injury to himself. The true nature of his complaint is clear. He says himself (p. 70) that Mr. Darwin did not think him worth notice and did not venture to attack him openly. This is the whole point and substance of his argument. The obvious truth is that his vanity has been wounded. When he saw the book advertised, he expected a formal reply. He found only the allusion at the end of Krause's article, and the reference to the book in the preface. When he discovered the inaccuracy, he immediately assumed that there must be malice. There was a plot to injure him by underhand methods. How else could anybody fail to give a serious reply to so terrible an antagonist?

This is really his whole case. If any change were to be introduced in consequence, it would not be in any way to *Butler's* advantage. The whole point of it would be to relieve *Mr. Darwin* from a possible imputation. It would do Butler no good, but it would deprive him of a pretext for charging Mr. Darwin with ill faith.

The whole question, therefore, to my mind comes to this: whether it is worth while for Mr. Darwin to do anything more than he has done in order to avoid this possible misconstruction? I say no, first because Mr. Darwin has done quite enough already and has given ample publicity to the facts. Secondly, because the misconstruction is so absurd that nobody could fall into it, unless he were blinded by wounded vanity. It is not conceivable that Mr.

Darwin wished to sink the fact of Butler having attacked him, for he mentions Butler's book: not that he thought him worth a serious answer, for he only publishes Krause's contemptuous reference: and the slip of the pen upon wh. this absurd theory rests is acknowledged in a letter published in the *Athenæum*, and in Butler's own book. I cannot think, therefore, that the correction is necessary in Mr. Darwin's interest, nor is it called for by justice to Butler: and to make any more fuss about such an infinitesimal detail would look like a consciousness of some appreciable injustice.   LESLIE STEPHEN

The following letter was written in 1904 when Mrs. Litchfield was preparing her *Emma Darwin* for the press. The inclusion of some account of the Samuel Butler misunderstanding was evidently under discussion, and though Frank had all along advised coming into the open with a fuller explanation than was given at the time, at this date—twenty-four years after the original rift—he is recommending reticence. Probably he considered that the letters suggested for inclusion would not in themselves give a fair view of the whole incident.

LETTER L, SEE P. 161

Francis Darwin to Henrietta Litchfield his sister

Jan. 23, '04   11, *Egerton Place, S.W.*
Dear Hen,
    . . . I should say the Butler row might be left out with great advantage. I left it all out of *More Letters*.—There was a sort of truce between Butler and our side, and now he is dead; and after all I now think he had some cause of complaint though he entirely lost his head and behaved abominably. Huxley's letter is good and I quite understand your liking to publish it. But I still think I would leave it out . . . I am almost sure that L. Huxley consulted

me about referring to Butler in his *Life of T. H. H.*, and that I asked
him not to. If so it would hardly do to print T. H. H.'s letter now.

I see there is no mention of Butler in Huxley's *Life* which I
have now looked at. . . .

Yr. Affec., F. D.

No mention of the quarrel is made in *Emma Darwin*.

So in the end Francis Darwin, Charles's biographer, thought
Butler had a real cause of complaint. The above documents which
passed to and fro amongst the Generals of the Darwin camp, must
help posterity to judge the protagonists, remote from the field of
battle. The turmoil of indecision behind the scenes, and the anxiety to do the proper thing, give a picture in these letters of an age
gone by; in Darwin's quiet Headquarters at Down, there was time
for irresolution and the writing of letters; whilst the rallying of
relations and friends to give him unanimous support reflects his
endearing gentle qualities.

Butler foresaw in the last lines of his Sonnet, that the ghost of
his quarrel with Darwin would not soon be laid. For even on the
"lips of living men" these two Victorian figures cannot be wholly
reconciled. Both were rebels against contemporary opinion; Butler stands as the perpetual revolutionary, who only turned against
Darwin after Darwin had become the acknowledged prophet.
Darwin was rebelling against current biological concepts and
delivered Man into the evolutionary machine; he rejected all easy
speculators as ephemeral, and to him Butler and his theories
remained ephemeral. Indeed in *Life and Habit* Butler had gone to
perverse and deliberate lengths to define his anti-scientific position. He wrote:—"I know nothing about science, and it is well
that there should be no mistake on this head; I neither know, nor
want to know, more detail than is necessary to enable me to give
a fairly broad and comprehensive view of my subject."

Butler's satirical genius lashed the shams and hypocrisies of his time. His writings on quasi-scientific themes as well as his philosophy on the art of living, were based on his inward experience, in revolt against fact-finding materialism. In Natural Selection and its dependence on chance variation for its effectiveness,—though Darwin himself vacillated on this point as Butler very well knew,—Butler saw a complete surrender to a mechanical world, with Man as the supreme machine, and all effect of Mind and its striving ruled out as a guiding force. He formed his theory of Mind and Memory in the speculative manner of the previous century, following and extending the ideas of Lamarck and Dr. Erasmus Darwin, with acknowledged indebtedness to his own contemporary, Dr. Hering. Butler paraded the old theories in a new guise, and took on the role of the maltreated, posthumous "enfant terrible" of the Physico-theologians of the 18th century. Butler's intervention into the scientific fold with this hybrid of science and philosophy could not be tolerated by the new biological school of Darwin and Huxley.

There is a close connection between this quarrel and Darwin's two disclaimers that I have discussed earlier; firstly his rejection of his grandfather's influence on his own views, and secondly his half-hearted denial that ideas of evolution were "in the air." But it was the force of Charles Darwin's simplicity and single-minded scientific purpose that binds these three affairs together; he rejected his grandfather's influence because he rejected Erasmus Darwin's speculative method; he denied that evolutionary ideas were ripening, because these floating ideas were not yet substantiated by evidence; and he found Butler's writing of no importance because Butler again did not look to the facts. For Charles Darwin had become the conscious exponent of evolutionary theory in a new form, and watched in his last years the beginnings of its application to wider fields of knowledge. Old facts had to be re-examined to understand their evolutionary sense; Darwin himself undertook his botanical work to look for this new meaning in botanical detail. His repudiation of those who spin their theories without the constant discipline of factual detail, was the inevitable concomitant of his scientific faith.

REFERENCES TO OTHER WORKS

Memoir of Samuel Butler, in two volumes. By Henry Festing Jones. Macmillan & Co., 1919. The quarrel is dealt with at great length, and contains the substance of the 1911 pamphlet, here reprinted.

Charles Darwin, the Fragmentary Man, by Geoffrey West. Routledge & Co., 1937.

Samuel Butler, a mid-Victorian Modern, by C. G. Stillman. Martin Secker, 1932.

Both contain good short summaries of the quarrel.

The Earnest Atheist, a Study of Samuel Butler, by Malcolm Muggeridge. Eyre and Spottiswoode, 1936.

Life and Letters of Charles Darwin, in three volumes, by Francis Darwin. John Murray, 1887. Has only the briefest mention of the quarrel in Vol. III, p. 220, and there is no mention of Samuel Butler in *More Letters*.

Samuel Butler states his case in the following books, besides his letters to the *Athenæum* and *Nature*. *Life and Habit*, 1877. *Evolution Old and New*, 1879. *Unconscious Memory*, 1880. *Luck or Cunning?* 1885–6.

Dr. Robert Darwin, from a contemporary silhouette
Circa 1826

Charles Darwin aged 33, with his eldest child, William
From a daguerreotype in the possession of
Sir Charles Darwin, Cambridge

Charles Darwin aged 51
(from a photograph by Maull & Fox)

Charles Darwin aged 72, on the verandah at Down, ready
for his customary stroll to the Sandwalk
(from a photograph by Elliott & Fry)

NOTES

NOTE ONE

Letter from Dr. Erasmus Darwin to his son Robert, Charles's father

THE FOLLOWING unpublished letter from Dr. Erasmus Darwin to his son Robert, Charles's father, throws light on the blunt, direct character of Erasmus and gives his views on some medical questions and on alcoholism and its transmission. I include it here as it shows on what terms the father and son were; the letter is an answer to what must have been an enquiry from Robert into the facts about his own mother's death and about his grandfather, Mr. Howard. In 1792, when this letter was written, Erasmus was sixty-one, the first Mrs. Darwin, Robert's mother, had been dead twenty-two years and Erasmus had re-married. Robert was twenty-six, and four years later he married Susannah Wedgwood, Charles's mother, so it is probable that his letter of enquiry had some eugenic intention, as his father clearly saw.

Derby Jan 5 [1792]

Dear Robert

I do not remember your having before asked me the questions about Mr. Howard and your mother; which I am sure I would openly without any scruple have answered. The late Mr. Howard was never to my knowledge in the least insane, he was a drunkard both in public and private—and when he went to London he became connected with a woman and lived a deba[u]ched life in respect to drink, hence he had always the Gout of which he died but without any the least symptom of either insanity or epilepsy, but from debility of digestion and Gout as other drunkards die.

In respect to your mother, the following is the true history, which I shall neither aggravate nor diminish anything. Her mind was truly amiable and her person handsome, which you may perhaps in some measure remember.

She was seized with pain on the left side about the lower edge of the liver, this pain was followed in about an hour by violent convulsions, and these sometimes relieved by great doses of opium, and some wine, which induced intoxication. At other times a temporary dilirium, or what by some might be termed insanity, came on for half an hour, and then she became herself again, and the paroxysm was terminated. This disease is called hysteria by some people. I think it allied to epilepsy.

This kind of disease had several returns in the course of 4 or 6 years and she then took to drinking spirit and water to relieve the pain, and I found (when it was too late) that she had done this in great quantity, the liver became swelled, and she gradually sunk, a few days before her death, she bled at the mouth, and whenever she had a scratch, as some hepatic patients do.

All the drunken diseases are hereditary in some degree, and I believe epilepsy and insanity are produced originally by drinking. I have seen epilepsy produced so very often—one sober generation cures these dr[unkards] frequently, which one drunken one has created.

I now know many families, who had insanity in one side, and the children now old people have no symptom of it. *If it was otherwise, there would not be a family in the kingdom without epileptic gouty or insane people in it.*

I well remember when your mother fainted away in these hysteric fits (which she often did) that she told me, you, who was not then 2 or 2 1/2 years old, run into the kitchen to call the maid-servant to her assistance.

I have told everything just as I recollect it, as I think it a matter of no consequence to yourself or your brother, who both live temperate lives, keeping betwixt all extreams.

I have lately taken to drink two glasses of home-made wine with water at my dinner, instead of water alone, as I found myself growing weak about two months ago; but am recovered and only now feel the approaches of old age.

I shall not mention your letter to Erasmus, you may always depend on secrecy when you require it.

My next book will come out in May. Adieu

From your affectionate father

E. DARWIN

NOTE TWO

How Dr. Robert's objections to the Voyage
were overcome

AT THE beginning of his *Beagle* Journal Charles Darwin wrote an
account of how the Wedgwoods—and especially his Uncle
Josiah—turned the balance in favour of his acceptance of the position of Naturalist offered by Captain Fitz-Roy.

"I had been wandering about North Wales on a geological tour
with Professor Sedgwick when I arrived home on Monday 29th of
August. My sisters first informed me of the letters from Prof.
Henslow and Mr. Peacock offering to me the place in the *Beagle*
which I now fill. I immediately said I would go; but the next
morning, finding my Father so much averse to the whole plan, I
wrote to Mr. Peacock to refuse his offer. On the last day of August
I went to Maer, where everything soon bore a different appearance. I found every member of the family so strongly on my side,
that I determined to make another effort. In the evening I drew
up a list of my Father's objections, to which Uncle Jos wrote his
opinion and answer. This we sent off to Shrewsbury early the next
morning and I went out shooting. About 10 o'clock Uncle Jos
sent me a message to say he intended going to Shrewsbury and
offering to take me with him. When we arrived there, all things
were settled, and my Father most kindly gave his consent."

Here follow the letters sent back from Maer to Shrewsbury for
Dr. Robert's consideration.

(Maer) August 31st, 1831

My dear Father,

I am afraid I am going to make you again very uncomfortable—but upon consideration I think you will excuse me once again stating my opinions on the offer of the voyage. My excuse and reason is the different way all the Wedgwoods view the subject from what you and my sisters do.

I have given Uncle Jos, what I fervently trust is an accurate and full list of your objections, and he is kind enough to give his opinion on all. The list and his answers will be enclosed, but may I beg of you one favour, it will be doing me the greatest kindness if you will send me a decided answer—Yes or No—; If the latter I should be most ungrateful if I did not implicitly yield to your better judgment and to the kindest indulgence which you have shown me all through my life,—and you may rely upon it I will never mention the subject again; if your answer should be Yes, I will go directly to Henslow and consult deliberately with him and then come to Shrewsbury. The danger appears to me and all the Wedgwoods not great—the expence cannot be serious, and the time I do not think anyhow, would be more thrown away than if I staid at home.—But pray do not consider that I am so bent on going, that I would for one single *moment* hesitate if you thought that after a short period you should continue uncomfortable.—I must again state I cannot think it would unfit me hereafter for a steady life.—I do hope this letter will not give you much uneasiness.—I send it by the car tomorrow morning; if you make up your mind directly will you send me an answer on the following day by the same means. If this letter should not find you at home, I hope you will answer as soon as you conveniently can.—

I do not know what to say about Uncle Jos' kindness, I never can forget how he interests himself about me.

Believe me, my dear Father,

Your affectionate son, CHARLES DARWIN

These were Dr. Robert's objections to the voyage, as reported to Uncle Jos by Charles.

1. Disreputable to my character as a Clergyman hereafter.
2. A wild scheme.
3. That they must have offered to many others before me the place of Naturalist.
4. And from its not being accepted there must be some serious objection to the vessel or expedition.
5. That I should never settle down to a steady life hereafter.
6. That my accommodations would be most uncomfortable.
7. That you, that is, Dr. Darwin, should consider it as again changing my profession.
8. That it would be a useless undertaking.

Also enclosed, was Josiah's letter to Dr. Robert, with "Read this last" in Charles's handwriting.

Maer, August 31st, 1831

My dear Doctor,

I feel the responsibility of your application to me on the offer that has been made to Charles. . . . Charles has put down what he conceives to be your principle objections, and I think the best course I can take will be to state what occurs to me upon each of them.

1. I should not think it would be in any degree disreputable to his character as a Clergyman. I should on the contrary think the offer honourable to him; and the pursuit of Natural History, though certainly not professional, is very suitable to a clergyman.
2. I hardly know how to meet this objection, but he would have definite objects upon which to employ himself, and might acquire and strengthen habits of application, and I should think would be as likely to do so as in any way in which he is likely to pass the next two years at home.

3. The notion did not occur to me in reading the letters; and on reading them again with that object in my mind I see no ground for it.

4. I cannot conceive that the Admiralty would send out a bad vessel on such a service. As to objections to the expedition, they will differ in each man's case, and nothing would, I think, be inferred in Charles's case, if it were known that others had objected.

5. You are a much better judge of Charles's character than I can be. If on comparing this mode of spending the next two years with the way in which he will probably spend them if he does not accept this offer, you think him more likely to be rendered [un]steady, and unable to settle, it is undoubtedly a weighty objection. Is it not the case that sailors are prone to settle in domestic and quiet habits?

6. I can form no opinion on this further than that if appointed by the Admiralty he will have a claim to be as well accommodated as the vessel will allow.

7. If I saw Charles now absorbed in professional studies I should probably think it would not be advisable to interrupt them; but this is not, and I think, will not be the case with him. His present pursuit of knowledge is in the same track as he would have to follow in the expedition.

8. The undertaking would be useless as regards his profession, but looking upon him as a man of enlarged curiosity, it affords him such an opportunity of seeing men and things as happens to few. You will bear in mind that I have had very little time for consideration, and that you and Charles are the persons who must decide.

> I am, my dear Doctor,
> Affectionately yours,
> JOSIAH WEDGWOOD

NOTE THREE

The pencil notes of 1837–38: "This is the Question"

THE FOLLOWING notes in Charles Darwin's hand were hurriedly scrawled in pencil on scraps of paper; one is on a letter addressed to him whilst he was living at 36 Great Marlborough Street. The writing of the notes must therefore have been in one of the years 1837 or '38. He was married to Emma Wedgwood on January 29th, 1839. How these youthful questionings escaped destruction cannot now be known. Perhaps they fell into the hands of Emma herself?

WORK FINISHED

If *not* marry TRAVEL? Europe—Yes? America????
If I travel it must be exclusively geological — United States — Mexico.

Depend upon health and vigour and how far I become zoological. If I don't travel—Work at transmission of Species—microscope—simplest forms of life—Geology—? Oldest formations?? Some experiments—physiological observations on lower animals.

(B). Live in London—for where else possible—in small house near Regents Park—keep horses—take Summer tours collect specimens some line of Zoolog: speculations of

WORK FINISHED

If marry—means limited—Feel duty to work for money. London life, nothing but Society, no country, no tours, no large Zoolog: collect., no books. — Cambridge Professorship, either Geolog: or Zoolog:—comply with all above requisites—I couldn't systematize zoologically so well.
But better than hibernating in country—and where? Better even than near London country house—I could not indolently take country house and do nothing—Could I live in London like a prisoner? If I were moderately rich I would live in London, with pretty big house and do as (B)—but could I act thus with

Geograph: range and geological general works—systematize and study affinities.

children and poor—? No— Then where live in country near London; better; but great obstacles to science and poverty.

Then Cambridge, better, but fish out of water, not being Professor and poverty. Then Cambridge Professorship,—and make best of it— do duty as such and work at spare times—My destiny will be Camb. Prof. or poor man; outskirts of London—some small square etc.—and work as well as I can.

I have so much more pleasure in direct observation, that I could not go on as Lyell does, correcting and adding up new information to old train, and I do not see what line can be followed by man tied down to London.—In country—experiment and observations on lower animals,—more space—

The second paper is headed:—*This is the Question*

MARRY	NOT MARRY
Children—(if it please God)—constant companion, (friend in old age) who will feel interested in one, object to be beloved and played with—better than a dog anyhow— Home, and someone to take care of house—Charms of music and female chit-chat. These things good for one's health. Forced to visit and receive relations *but terrible loss of time.*	No children, (no second life) no one to care for one in old age.—What is the use of working without sympathy from near and dear friends— who are near and dear friends to the old except relatives.
	Freedom to go where one liked— Choice of Society *and little of it.* Conversation of clever men at clubs.—
My God, it is intolerable to think of spending one's whole life, like a neuter bee, working, working and	Not forced to visit relatives, and to bend in every trifle—to have the expense and anxiety of children— perhaps quarrelling.

nothing after all.—No, no won't do.—

Imagine living all one's day solitarily in smoky dirty London House.—Only picture to yourself a nice soft wife on a sofa with good fire, and books and music perhaps—compare this vision with the dingy reality of Grt Marlboro' St. Marry—Marry—Marry Q.E.D.

Loss of time—cannot read in the evenings—fatness and idleness—anxiety and responsibility—less money for books etc—if many children forced to gain one's bread.— (But then it is very bad for one's health to work too much)

Perhaps my wife won't like London; then the sentence is banishment and degradation with indolent idle fool—

On the reverse side of the page comes the summing up

It being proved necessary to marry—When? Soon or Late. The Governor says soon for otherwise bad if one has children—one's character is more flexible—one's feelings more lively, and if one does not marry soon, one misses so much good pure happiness.—

But then if I married tomorrow: there would be an infinity of trouble and expense in getting and furnishing a house,—fighting about no Society—morning calls—awkwardness—loss of time every day—(without one's wife was an angel and made one keep industrious)—Then how should I manage all my business if I were obliged to go every day walking with my wife.—Eheu!! I never should know French,—or see the Continent,—or go to America, or go up in a Balloon, or take solitary trip in Wales—poor slave, you will be worse than a negro—And then horrid poverty (without one's wife was better than an angel and had money)—Never mind my boy—Cheer up—One cannot live this solitary life, with groggy old age, friendless and cold and childless staring one in one's face, already beginning to wrinkle. Never mind, trust to chance—keep a sharp look out.—There is many a happy slave—

NOTE FOUR

Mrs. Darwin's papers on Religion

COPIES OF two letters written by Mrs. Darwin to her husband, both annotated by him, found amongst her papers after her death. The first, undated, is on a sheet of old-fashioned note-paper, and was written shortly after their marriage, as Charles Darwin states in the *Autobiography*. The second was written in or before 1861, when Charles dated his added note. Mrs. Darwin's writing is neat and without corrections, suggesting a copy from a draft. Written at the end of each are a few lines by Charles Darwin.

LETTER ONE

The state of mind that I wish to preserve with respect to you, is to feel that while you are acting conscientiously and sincerely wishing and trying to learn the truth, you cannot be wrong, but there are some reasons that force themselves upon me, and prevent myself from being always able to give myself this comfort. I daresay you have often thought of them before, but I will write down what has been in my head, knowing that my own dearest will indulge me. Your mind and time are full of the most interesting subjects and thoughts of the most absorbing kind, viz. following up your own discoveries—but which make it very difficult for you to avoid casting out as interruptions other sorts of thoughts which have no relation to what you are pursuing, or to be able to give your whole attention to both sides of the question.

There is another reason which would have a great effect on a woman, but I don't know whether it wd. so much on a man. I mean E.[125] whose understanding you have such a very high opinion of and whom you have so much affection for, having gone before you—is it not likely to have made it easier to you and to have taken off some of that dread fear which the feeling of doubting first gives and which I do not think an unreasonable or superstitious feeling. It seems to me also that the line of your pursuits may have led you to view chiefly the difficulties on one side, and that you have not had time to consider and study the chain of difficulties on the other, but I believe you do not consider your opinion as formed. May not the habit in scientific pursuits of believing nothing till it is proved, influence your mind too much in other things which cannot be proved in the same way, and which if true are likely to be above our comprehension. I should say also there is a danger in giving up revelation which does not exist on the other side, that is the fear of ingratitude in casting off what has been done for your benefit as well as for that of all the world and which ought to make you still more careful, perhaps even fearful lest you should not have taken all the pains you could to judge truly. I do not know whether this is arguing as if one side were true and the other false, which I meant to avoid, but I think not. I do not quite agree with you in what you once said that luckily there were no doubts as to how one ought to act. I think prayer is an instance to the contrary, in one case it is a positive duty and perhaps not in the other. But I daresay you meant in actions which concern others and then I agree with you almost if not quite. I do not wish for any answer to all this—it is a satisfaction to me to write it, and when I talk to you about it I cannot say exactly what I wish to say, and I know you will have patience with your own dear wife. Don't think that it is not

---

[125] Erasmus, Charles's elder brother. She means that Erasmus had preceded Charles in the matter of doubt and unbelief.—N. B.

my affair and that it does not much signify to me. Everything
that concerns you concerns me and I should be most unhappy if
I thought we did not belong to each other for ever. I am rather
afraid my own dear Nigger will think I have forgotten my promise not to bother him, but I am sure he loves me, and I cannot
tell him how happy he makes me and how dearly I love him and
thank him for all his affection which makes the happiness of my
life more and more every day.

> When I am dead, know
> that many times, I
>   have kissed and cryed
>   over this. C. D.

LETTER TWO

I cannot tell you the compassion I have felt for all your suffering for these weeks past that you have had so many drawbacks.
Nor the gratitude I have felt for the cheerful and affectionate
looks you have given me when I know you have been miserably
uncomfortable.

My heart has often been too full to speak or take any notice. I
am sure you know I love you well enough to believe that I mind
your suffering nearly as much as I should my own and I find the
only relief to my own mind is to take it as from God's hand, and
to try to believe that all suffering and illness is meant to help us
to exalt our minds and to look forward with hope to a future state.
When I see your patience, deep compassion for others, self command and above all gratitude for the smallest thing done to help
you I cannot help longing that these precious feelings should be
offered to Heaven for the sake of your daily happiness. But I find
it difficult enough in my own case. I often think of the words

"Thou shalt keep him in perfect peace whose mind is stayed on thee." It is feeling and not reasoning that drives one to prayer.

I feel presumptuous in writing this to you. I feel in my inmost heart your admirable qualities and feelings and all I would hope is that you would direct them upwards, as well as to one who values them above everything in the world. I shall keep this by me till I feel cheerful and comfortable again about you but it has passed through my mind often lately so I thought I would write it partly to relieve my own mind.

.   .   .

God Bless you C. D. 1861

These letters are printed in *Emma Darwin*, Vol. II, John Murray, 1915 pp. 173–176. Mrs. Litchfield writes of her mother:—

In our childhood and youth she was not only sincerely religious—this she always was in the true sense of the word—but definite in her beliefs. She went regularly to church and took the Sacrament. She read the Bible with us and taught us a simple Unitarian Creed, though we were baptized and confirmed in the Church of England. In her youth religion must have largely filled her life, and there is evidence in the papers she left that it distressed her in her early married life to know that my father did not share her faith. She wrote two letters to him on the subject. He speaks in his autobiography of "her beautiful letter to me, safely preserved, shortly after our marriage."

NOTE FIVE

On Charles Darwin's Ill-Health

HEALTH ANXIETIES haunt the pages of the *Autobiography*, yet Charles Darwin's many medical advisers never reached definite conclusions as to the cause of his long bouts of illness. No diagnosis was ever made of a causal organic disorder. Since his death biographers and doctors alike have discussed the emphasis on ill-health, so apparent in his own personal writings and in those of Emma his wife, but there remains no concensus of opinion as to the cause of his symptoms. The nausea, giddyness, insomnia and debility from which he suffered, follow the now familiar pattern of the ills of other eminent Victorians, with the Victorian Hydropathic Establishment, the sofa and the shawl as characteristic hallmarks. Charles Darwin's forty years of invalid existence, moreover, were an unexpected sequel to his youthful vigour, for his strength and endurance were well above the average, as Captain Fitz-Roy has recorded in his accounts of various incidents during the *Beagle* Voyage.

Yet health anxieties did trouble Charles Darwin even in the early days before the voyage, so that his marriage to a deeply sympathetic wife can hardly have done more than increase a deep-seated tendency. Her over-solicitude helped to cast that faint aura of glory on the Symptom, an attitude that was carried on into adult life by several of their children.

Many theories have been put forward to account for Darwin's years of suffering, ranging from the possibility of appendicitis, a duodenal ulcer, pyorrhea, or the damaging effects of sea-sickness during the voyage; but recent emphasis has been in the direction of neurotic or psychotic causes.

I am not qualified to discuss these different points of view, but I give references and very brief summaries for those who may want to explore this field further.

1. ALVAREZ, Walter C., M.D. *Nervousness, Indigestion and Pain.* Paul B. Hoeber Inc. Medical Book Department of Harper Bros., New York and London. 7th printing. 1947.

   Dr. Alvarez examines the symptoms of Darwin's illness, and deduces from the fact that no physician could discover any organic source, that "his troubles were functional and due to an inherited peculiarity of the nervous system." He found evidence of psychological instability among his ancestors, and concludes that he had a "poor nervous heredity on both sides."

2. BARLOW, N. *Lancet*, i, 1954, p. 414. (See also 3(a) and 4, (c) and (d).)

3. GOOD, Dr. Rankine. (a) *Lancet*, i, 1954, p. 106. Also (b) "The Origin of the Origin." *Biology and Human Affairs*, Oct. 1954.

   Dr. Good kindly let me read his typescript entitled "The Psychology of the Revolutionary," before it appeared in shorter form in *Biology and Human Affairs*.

   Dr. Good finds that Charles Darwin's illness "was compounded of depressive, obsessional, anxiety and hysterical symptoms, which for the most part co-existed. . . ." He finds "evidence that unmistakably points" to these symptoms being a "distorted expression of the aggression, hate, resentment, felt at an unconscious level, by Darwin towards his tyrannical father . . ." In Dr. Good's opinion, his forty years of ill-health were the punishment for his revolt.

4. HUBBLE, Dr. Douglas. (a) *Lancet*, 1943, i, p. 129. (b) *Horizon*, LXXX, 1946, p. 74. (c) *Lancet*, ii, 1953, p. 1351. (d) *Lancet*, i, 1954, p. 467.

In 1946 Dr. Hubble wrote:—"Charles Darwin's illness, then, arose from the suppression and non-recognition of a painful emotion. Such an emotion is always compounded of fear, guilt or hate . . . in Charles Darwin this emotion arose from his relationship with his father." In the last two references Dr. Hubble has added to this theme, and references 4, (c), entitled "The Life of the Shawl," gave rise to the discussion in the Lancet under the same title.

5. KEMPF, E. J. *Psychopathology*. London, 1921, p. 208.

Dr. Kempf takes Charles Darwin's medical history to show that affective cravings brought about by resistence to parental coercion cause after-anxiety; these demonstrate the mechanisms, in his view, "of the prolonged struggles to sublimate affective needs." Dr. Kempf stresses the loss of Charles's mother, who died when he was eight years old. Kempf also stresses Dr. Robert Darwin's authoritarian attitude towards his family, noting at the same time his unusual insight in dealing with patients. Kempf says:—"he practised the present psychoanalytical principle of inducing an affective catharsis and readjustment in his patients as a method of treating the distress caused by affective suppression-anxiety."

It seems as though the last word has not yet been written on the problem of Charles Darwin's ill-health. One thing is clear; he realised with deep insight how his own profit and loss account stood when he wrote near the end of the *Autobiography*:—"Even ill-health, though it has annihilated several years of my life, has saved me from the distractions of society and amusement."

NOTE SIX

Page and line references to the more important previously omitted passages

Minus numerals indicate lines from bottom of page

p. 21, line 12 to line 15. "I have heard . . . my case."

p. 21, line -4 to line -1. "I believe . . . invalid state."

p. 22, line 1 to line 3. "Before going . . . plan answered."

p. 22, line 5 to line 10. "Caroline was . . . she might say."

p. 23, line 9 to line -1. "About this time . . . run so fast!"

p. 28, line -17 to p. 29, line 5. "My Father . . . patient bled."

p. 29, line 13 to line -6. "Family quarrels . . . ever afterwards."

p. 30, line -3 to p. 31, line 5. "A connection . . . least know."

p. 38, line 6 to line 9. "nor to my . . . whole lives."

p. 38, line 12 to line 14. "The above sketch . . . no merit."

p. 39, line -12 to line -10. "Some of . . . distinguished."

p. 42, line -7 to line -6. "but was superficial . . . tongue."

p. 46, line -15 to line -14. "He had . . . gentleman."

p. 49, line 13 to line 17. "It never struck . . . incredibile."

p. 56, line -2 to p. 57, line 2. "At first . . . humour."

p. 62, line 3 to line 5. "This was shown . . . offended him."

p. 62, line 8 to line 13. "The junior . . . common sense."

p. 62, line -14. "for when . . . unreasonable."

p. 63, line 3 to p. 64, line -12. "I remember . . . appearance."

p. 64, line -10. "though . . . blemishes."

p. 66, line 14 to line 15. "The primeval . . . civilised man."

p. 70, line 14. "facile . . . botanicorum."

p. 71, line -12 to line -8. "from its manifestly . . . barbarian."

p. 72, line 12 to line 15. "Beautiful . . . allegories."

p. 72, line -8 to line -1. "and have never . . . doctrine."

p. 73, line 11 to line 12. "Everything . . . laws."

p. 75, line 17 to line -13. "A being . . . endless time?"

p. 75, line -5 to p. 76, line 4. "But it cannot . . . to arise."

p. 77, line -6 to p. 78, line 2. "May not these . . . a snake."

p. 78, line 6 to p. 80, line 13. "A man who has no assured . . . Redeemer liveth."

p. 80, line -12 to p. 81, line -8. "You all know . . . sweet ways."

p. 83, line -11 to line -9. "On such . . . standing up."

p. 84, line 4 to line 15. "He had . . . strength failed."

p. 84, line -2 to p. 85, line -3. "All the leading . . . glory."

p. 85, line -1 to p. 86, line 1. "and before . . . morning."

p. 86, line 3 to line 4. "He never . . . biology."

p. 86, line 12 to line 14. "who was . . . five years,"

p. 86, line 14 to line -12. "I suppose . . . this country."

p. 86, line -6 to p. 88, line -5. "He was rather . . . mankind."

p. 89, line 3 to line 7. "He was very . . . dirty."

p. 89, line 14 to p. 90, line -9. "I used to call . . . Speaking of H. Spencer."

p. 91, line 5 to line 6. "H. Spencer . . . of it!"

p. 91, line 12 to line 13. "What he . . . conversation."

p. 92, line -10 to line -6. "I met . . . very premature."

p. 92, line -4 to line -1. "I have heard . . . whom I knew,"

p. 94, line -2. "who never . . . they can."

p. 95, line 10 to line 19. "Whilst I was . . . children."

p. 103, line 14 to line -13. "I must, however . . . lawyer."

p. 106, line 6 to line 7. "on the . . . Cucurbitacean plant."

p. 110, line 10 to line -9. "Owing . . . Louse."

p. 117, line -13 to line -9. "I informed . . . be sold."

p. 118. The last sentence in italics.

INDEX